Alison Burt

Illustrated by Helen Youens

Edited by
Kathleen Blayney

Designed by
Keith Groom and Cyril Mason

Mills & Boon Limited
London

This edition published 1976 by
Mills and Boon Limited,
17–19 Foley Street, London W1A 1DR

ISBN 0 263 06013 6

© Sackett Publishing Services Ltd. 1975

Filmset by Ramsay Typesetters
(Crawley) Ltd, through Reynolds Clark
Associates Ltd, London
Printed in Italy by New Interlitho S.P.A.

Sure and Simple Series
created and produced by
Sackett Publishing Services Ltd,
104 Great Portland Street, London W1N 5PE

CONTENTS

Weights and Measures	6–7
Herbs and Spices	8–9
Soups	10–13
Eggs	14–21
Cheese	22–23
Fish	24–31
Meat	32–47
Vegetables	48–53
Pasta and Rice	54–57
Sauces	58–65
Cold Desserts	66–73
Hot Puddings	74–81
Fruit	82–83
Pastry	84–97
Scones	98–99
Cakes	100–109
Biscuits	110–111
Cooking with Yeast	112–115
Drinks	116–117
Preserving	118–125
Index	126
Acknowledgements	128

Measuring and Weighing

The recipes in this book are given in both Imperial and Metric measures. Simply follow each recipe using either set of measurements, but do not interchange them.

Until you are experienced in cooking, it is as well to measure accurately all the ingredients that you use. Ideally, buy some weighing scales. You will find them invaluable.

Measuring in Metric

Metric measures differ from the Imperial mainly in the terms used for the various weights, measurements and temperatures.

* Dry ingredients, fats, cheese, fruit, vegetables, meat and fish are weighed in grams (g) and kilograms (kg).
* Liquid ingredients are measured in millimetres (ml), decilitres (dl) and litres.
* Cake tins, some moulds and length measurements are measured in centimetres (cm).
* Oven temperatures are given in Celsius (°C) for electric cookers but the gas 'Marks' are the same.

Length measurements

The exact conversion to 1 inch is 2·54 cm. Rather than struggle with this cumbersome number, when converting inches to centimetres, use 1 inch to 2·5 cm.

Converting existing recipes to Metric measures

Soon all foodstuffs will be sold in metric packages and amounts. Weighing scales and measuring utensils, which at the moment have the dual Imperial and Metric scales, will eventually be entirely metric. For these reasons it is now necessary to convert existing recipes to metric measures.

Converting ounces and pounds to grams and kilograms is rather complicated. One ounce is equivalent to 28·35 g. Understandably, not many people could or have the time to cope with the cumbersome arithmetic involved with converting Imperial to exact Metric measurement. To simplify matters, use 25 g for each 1 oz. The slight discrepancy between the real and actual conversion does not make much difference, especially when using small quantities. The recipe will produce the same dish, only slightly smaller. Bear in mind that smaller cake tins may be needed and that the cooking time will have to be reduced a little. For many dishes, especially those which use large quantities, the difference may be too great. With dishes such as vegetables, roasts, stews and casseroles, fish etc . . . the size and number of the servings is important. For these recipes, multiply the ounces by 30 g then measure to the 25 g unit *below*, on your scales.

Liquid measures

One of the best features of metrication is that the dry and liquid measurements are consistent. One ounce can be converted to 25 g; 1 fluid oz can be converted to 25 ml. Follow this rule, multiplying fluid ounces by 25 ml, for recipes that rely on exact proportions of the ingredients for success — sauces, preserves, cakes, pastry etc. It is sometimes more exact however and more convenient to convert to decilitres (dl). A $\frac{1}{4}$ pint is exactly equal to 142 ml — to the nearest 25 ml unit, 150 ml — $1\frac{1}{2}$ dl.

Some measuring jugs have millilitres (ml) marked on the measuring scale, some decilitres (dl). Decilitres are very widely used as a measure in European countries. 1 dl is equal to 100 ml.

Spoon Measurements

ALL THE SPOON MEASUREMENTS IN THIS BOOK ARE LEVEL
The teaspoon has a capacity of 5 ml
The tablespoon has a capacity of 20 ml
Therefore, 4 teaspoons are equal to 1 tablespoon.

Handy Measures

1 slightly rounded tablespoon equals approximately: 1 oz/25 g sugar or rice.
1 rounded tablespoon equals approximately: 1 oz/25g flour, cornflour, custard powder or cocoa.

Australian Cup Measurements

In Australia, fewer people have weighing scales. Many cooks rely on cup measurements. The Australian cup has a capacity of 8 fluid oz/225 ml. The following chart will help these people.
1 cup equals approximately:
    3 oz/75 g desiccated coconut
    4 oz/100 g flour, grated cheese
    5 oz/150 g dried fruit, (sultanas, currants, raisins) brown sugar, sifted icing sugar
    6 oz/175 g semolina, ground rice
    7 oz/200 g caster sugar
    8 oz/225 g white sugar

Oven Temperatures

	Electricity	Electricity	Gas
Very slow	225°F	110°C	$\frac{1}{4}$
	250°F	130°C	$\frac{1}{2}$
Slow	275°F	140°C	1
	300°F	150°C	2
Moderately slow	325°F	170°C	3
Moderate	350°F	180°C	4
Moderately hot	375°F	190°C	5
Hot	400°F	200°C	6
	425°F	220°C	7
Very hot	450°F	230°C	8
	475°F	240°C	9

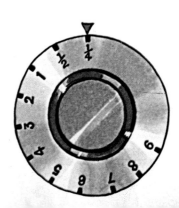

Herbs and Spices

If fresh herbs are available, do use them as the flavour is so much better than that of the dried. If the recipe says 1 level teaspoon dried herbs use 1 level tablespoon chopped fresh herbs. For a *bouquet garni* use 1 bay leaf, 2–3 parsley stalks and a sprig of thyme tied together You can buy convenient sachets of dried herbs which are called, and can be used in the same way as, a bouquet garni. The following herbs are the most readily available.

Herbs and spices are a necessity in any kitchen and very well worth growing in the garden or even in window boxes. They are the one means by which a cook gives a recipe originality and that special 'something' which makes the dish all her own. Some people know almost by instinct the right amount of herb or spice to add to a dish, some have to learn by experience. The most important point is that the herbs and spices should not be the predominant flavour, but should be used in relatively small amounts just to enhance the flavour of the dish. The exceptions to this rule are the hot dishes such as curry or chilli con carne, where the very heat of the spices gives the dish its name.

Bay Leaves: Good in almost any sauce, stew or casserole, when boiling meat or poaching fish. Add to kebabs and put in the dish while cooking a pâté.

Basil: Much used in Italian cooking: pizza toppings, pasta sauces. Especially good with any dish using tomatoes.

Chives: Mild oniony flavour. Mix into cheese dishes or snip over salads of all sorts.

Marjoram: Blends well in tomato dishes, including salads. Add a pinch to well-flavoured soups, casseroles and sauces. Ideal with lamb and pork.

Mint: Good with lamb. Add to new potatoes, spring carrots or peas while cooking.

Oregano: Very strong flavour, to be used with care in strong flavoured dishes. Much used in Italian cooking (see Basil) and tomato dishes.

Parsley: Use chopped or in sprigs for garnishing. Parsley sauce is good with broad beans, ham, white fish. Stalks have most flavour. Add to sauces, stews, casseroles, when boiling meat or poaching fish. Goes with most foods.

Rosemary: Very good with lamb, pork and veal. Sprinkle on to roasting meat or add to casseroles. Use with care.

Sage: Can be overpowering, so be careful. Use with cheese dishes. Good with pork and bacon. Sage and onion stuffing (see page 46).

Tarragon: Good with fish and eggs. Use in chicken, veal and game dishes.

Thyme: Very aromatic, use with care. Add to rabbit or chicken dishes. Parsley and thyme stuffing (see page 46).

Spices and Aromatic Seeds

These are widely used in both sweet and savoury dishes. Spices are usually bought ready ground but seeds are left whole.

Caraway seeds: Much used in Middle European cooking, e.g. Hungarian goulash, borsch (beetroot) soup, sauerkraut. Sprinkle on or add to bread, buns, cakes and biscuits.

Cayenne pepper: A very hot pepper which must be used with care. Add a pinch to cheese dishes, seafood cocktail and barbecue sauce.

Chilli powder: Very hot. An essential ingredient for Chilli con carne. Much used in Indian cooking.

Cinnamon: Good in sweet milky drinks. Especially good with chocolate flavour. Sprinkle on cakes, buns or stewed fruit. Good in glazes for boiled pork and bacon joints.

Cloves: Used whole as a flavouring while cooking boiled meat. Stud the fat of ham joints with whole cloves. Ground, add to spicy cakes, biscuits and puddings.

Ginger: Good with melon. Very good in curries and spicy stews. Essential for gingerbread, ginger snaps etc., also for homemade ginger beer.

Nutmeg: Very good in potato mixtures. Blends well with chocolate flavour. Sprinkle on top of milk puddings of all sorts. Add to breads and cakes.

Paprika: A mild sweet red pepper. Essential for goulash. Much used for garnishing because of its colour.

Pepper (Black and White): Use freshly ground for seasoning most dishes. Black has the better flavour.

Saffron: Used to flavour and colour rice. Essential for Cornish Saffron Buns. It is rather expensive.

Turmeric: Often used as a cheaper substitute for saffron but the flavour is inferior. Use in piccalilli, kedgeree and other Indian dishes.

Soups

Making soup is so easy that it is surprising more housewives don't do it. Perhaps the need for stock deters people, but even stock is simplicity itself to make. Stock cubes are not an ideal substitute. Broths are perhaps the most rewarding type of soup to make as they are a complete meal in themselves, with pieces of meat and vegetables. Purée and cream soups can be both elegant and homely, depending on the ingredients. Chilled soups are becoming more popular for summer parties. The most elegant soups are the consommés, which are really high class cooking, not family fare.

Stock

No one has a stockpot simmering on the cooker now, but more and more people are making and storing stock in their refrigerators and food freezers. Have a special bowl and add the vegetable stock (from cooking vegetables), the bone stock (from cooking up bones) and other cooking liquor as available. It is important to boil up the stock, all together, every three days. Don't add any actual pieces of meat, bones or vegetables or the stock may become sour. Don't have too much of one vegetable — the flavour will predominate. If you have some bones or a chicken to make into stock, flavour them as follows:

  1 lb/½ kg bones
  2 pints/1 litre water
  1 onion, peeled
  1 carrot, peeled
  bouquet garni (1 bay leaf, sprig of thyme, 2–3 parsley stalks, tied together)
  6 peppercorns
  ½ lemon (optional, for veal or chicken)

Chop the bones or ask the butcher to do this for you. Beef bones can be cooked in the oven to brown them first in order to make a good brown stock. Put the bones in a pan with a little meat if available to add flavour. Shin is a good meat to add, especially for beef stock. Add the other ingredients. Bring to the boil, then skim. If the froth is not taken off it may make the stock cloudy. Cover the pan and cook slowly for 2–3 hours. Strain and skim off any fat before using or storing.

NOTE: If you have a pressure cooker, about 30–45 minutes' cooking at 15 lb/6 kg pressure will be enough.

Chicken and Leek Broth
Serves 6

The chicken can be served in the soup or the broth served first, followed by the chicken as a main course. A rabbit could be used instead of the boiling fowl for a variation.

  1 small boiling fowl
  1 onion, peeled
  2 carrots, peeled
  3 pints/1¾ litres water or stock
  3 level tablespoons pearl barley, washed
  4 leeks, cleaned

Chop the chicken into 6 portions. Put all the ingredients, except the leeks, in a saucepan, bring to the boil and skim. Cover and simmer gently for 2 hours. Add the leeks and cook for 30 minutes more. Serve very hot.

Potato Soup   Serves 6

  1½ lb/¾ kg potatoes
  2 onions
  2 oz/50 g butter
  2½ pints/1½ litres stock
  salt and pepper
  ¼ pint/1½ dl milk
  grated cheese for garnish

Peel the potatoes and onions. Heat the butter in a saucepan and grate the potatoes and onions coarsely into it. Add the stock and seasonings. Bring to the boil, then cover the pan and simmer gently for 15–20 minutes, until the vegetables are very tender. Add the milk and re-heat. Adjust seasoning and serve sprinkled with grated cheese.

Cream Soups

Cream soup can be served for any occasion, the flavouring being chosen according to the vegetables which are in season and good value at the time. The more expensive vegetables, such as asparagus, make an ideal soup for entertaining. In the recipe below about 1 lb/$\frac{1}{2}$ kg other vegetables can be substituted for celery.

Cream of Celery Soup
Serves 6

A small amount of celery can be cooked and kept for adding to the soup just before serving. Cooked diced carrot makes a colourful garnish. Add a little cream just before serving if liked.

- 1 head celery
- 1 oz/25 g butter
- 1 oz/25 g plain flour
- 1$\frac{1}{2}$ pints/9 dl stock
- 1 teaspoon lemon juice
- pinch of grated nutmeg
- salt and pepper

Tomato Soup
Serves 6

Use fresh tomatoes if you prefer but they must be very red and ripe. Skin them before using. For special occasions add a little finely grated orange rind and some of the juice.

- 1 tablespoon olive oil
- 2 rashers streaky bacon, chopped
- 1 onion, chopped
- 1 carrot, chopped
- 1 stick celery, chopped
- 1 level tablespoon plain flour
- 1 (1 lb 4 oz/568 g) can tomatoes
- 1 dessert apple, peeled and grated
- 1 pint/6 dl stock
- 1 level tablespoon tomato purée
- $\frac{1}{2}$ level teaspoon dried basil
- 1 bay leaf

Heat the oil in a large saucepan and fry the bacon, stirring, until softened. Add the vegetables

1 Scrub the celery very well, then chop coarsely. Heat the butter in a large pan and cook the celery gently, stirring frequently, for 10 minutes. Sprinkle in the flour and cook, stirring, for 2–3 minutes.

2 Remove the pan from the heat and slowly blend in the stock. Add the lemon juice, nutmeg, salt and pepper. Bring to the boil, then reduce the heat and simmer gently for about 30 minutes or until the celery is very tender.

3 Either blend the soup in an electric blender until smooth or press it through a sieve with a wooden spoon. Reheat, add pieces of cooked celery, diced cooked carrot if available and a little cream if liked and serve piping hot.

and cook gently, stirring, for 5 minutes. Sprinkle in the flour and cook, still stirring, for 2–3 minutes. Blend in all the remaining ingredients. Bring to the boil, cover the pan, and simmer gently for 45 minutes. Remove the bay leaf, blend the cooked soup until smooth in an electric blender or press it through a sieve with a wooden spoon. Reheat, then taste and adjust the seasoning. Serve at once.

Gaspacho
Serves 4

A chilled summer soup from Spain which, naturally enough, is ideal to serve on hot sunny days. It would be excellent for a special luncheon party.

- $1\frac{1}{2}$ lb/675 g red ripe tomatoes, skinned
- $\frac{1}{2}$ onion, very finely chopped or grated
- 1 small green pepper, deseeded and chopped
- $\frac{1}{2}$ cucumber, peeled and chopped
- 1 clove garlic, crushed
- 6 tablespoons olive oil
- 3 tablespoons white wine vinegar
- $\frac{1}{4}$ pint/$1\frac{1}{2}$ dl chicken stock
- 1 small can tomato juice
- salt and freshly ground black pepper
- pinch of cayenne pepper
- chives or parsley for garnish
- 12 Spanish stuffed green olives, diced cucumber, croûtons of crisp fried bread, tomato and onion for serving

Quarter and deseed the tomatoes. Put with all other ingredients, except those for garnishing and serving and purée in two batches in an electric blender. Or put the prepared tomatoes into a bowl with onion, green pepper, cucumber and garlic. Blend in the olive oil, vinegar and stock, then the tomato juice. Season to taste. Chill for at least 30 minutes. Garnish with chopped chives or parsley.

Freezing Soup
Soups freeze well and are a good way of using vegetables which don't otherwise freeze well — celery, cucumber, lettuce and so on. Stock also is a good freezer standby. Before freezing, boil the completed and strained stock until it is very concentrated. Reconstitute for use. Freeze soup in usable quantities in plastic containers or pre-formed polythene bags (placed in sugar cartons to make a block shape). Remember to allow headspace for expansion, that is do not fill the containers quite full. Add any cream or egg yolk when reheating, to avoid separating or curdling.

All Purpose Eggs

Eggs are among the cook's best friends – so simple and yet so versatile. Boiled, poached, fried, baked, scrambled or in the form of omelettes, they make a meal in themselves, and they play a vital part in the preparation of countless other dishes. For instance, in cakes, sponges, meringues, soufflés, etc. they act as a raising agent because air has been beaten in with them. They are also used for binding dry ingredients together, as in rissoles, and for coating fried foods to protect them from the hot fat; and in mayonnaise egg yolks are used to emulsify the oil. Even the shells can be used to clarify consommés, and yolks and whites can of course be used separately. Whether you prefer brown or white eggs is immaterial – they are exactly the same quality inside. You may keep eggs in the refrigerator, but don't use them straight out of it for cooking. In the following pages we show you four principal ways of using eggs: on their own, in batters, in custards and finally meringues, soufflés and other dishes made mainly with egg whites.

Eggs on Their Own

Boiled: If your boiled eggs tend to crack in cooking, make sure they start at room temperature and remove the pan of boiling water from the heat before putting in the eggs. Keep the water boiling *slowly*. Time them to your requirements as follows: *Soft-boiled 3–4 minutes, firm 4–5, hard-boiled 10 minutes.*

Fried: Again use eggs at room temperature. Heat at least $\frac{1}{8}$ inch/ $\frac{1}{4}$ cm fat or oil in the pan, but see that it is not too hot when you add the eggs. Spoon a little hot oil over the yolks to set them. Eggs sometimes stick to the pan because bacon has just been cooked in it, leaving a deposit of salt.

Poached: Break the eggs carefully and slip one by one into a frying pan half full of boiling water. Use special poaching rings to keep the eggs in shape. Simmer for 3–5 minutes until the eggs are as firm as you like them. Serve on hot buttered toast.

Baked Eggs   Serves 4

Eggs 'en cocotte', that is, baked in small individual ovenproof dishes, make an elegant light lunch or supper. For a more substantial dish, extra ingredients can be cooked under the eggs – for instance, try it with ratatouille (see page 49). For a variation, try baking the eggs in a hollowed out vegetable. Try halved baked potatoes, aubergines (egg plant) or large tomatoes.

    4 oz/100 g butter
    4–8 eggs
    salt and pepper
    4 tablespoons thin cream (optional)

Heat the oven to 325°F/170°C/ Mark 3. Butter 4 small ovenproof dishes. Add 1 or 2 eggs to each dish and sprinkle with salt and pepper. Dot the remaining butter over the eggs. Pour 1 tablespoon cream into each dish. Bake the eggs for about 10 minutes or until just set – the white will still be creamy. Serve at once.

Scrambled Eggs and Omelettes

Scrambled eggs and omelettes start with almost the same mixture – the difference is in the cooking. For scrambled eggs:

1 Beat the eggs lightly, add salt and pepper to taste and 1 tablespoon milk for each egg.

2 Melt a little butter or margarine in a saucepan (about $\frac{1}{2}$ oz/15 g for 2 eggs). Add the eggs and cook very slowly over low heat, stirring all the time with a wooden spoon until the mixture is thick but still creamy. If it is overcooked it will be dry.

3 Have hot buttered toast ready for serving, as scrambled egg cools very quickly. Garnish with a sprig of parsley if liked.

For an omelette the egg is mixed with a little water instead of milk and it is cooked very quickly without stirring and finally folded over (see directions opposite).

French Omelette   Serves 1

Simplest and quickest of all to make and many flavourings and fillings can be added. For an omelette 'aux fines herbes' add 1 level teaspoon mixed dried herbs to the eggs when whisking. Cheese, cooked mushrooms, cooked bacon, vegetables, etc. can be added just before it is folded.

2 eggs
2 teaspoons water
salt and pepper
$\frac{1}{4}$ oz/7 g butter

Break the eggs into a bowl, add the water, salt and pepper. Beat together well but not so much that the eggs become watery. Heat the butter in a 6 inch/15 cm omelette pan until sizzling hot but not browned. Add the eggs to the pan and cook quickly. Using a fork, draw the cooked egg from around the edge to the centre of the pan so that uncooked egg can run into the space. When cooked, the omelette will be set underneath but still creamy on top. Add any filling, then fold the omelette over, out of the pan onto a serving plate. Serve straight away

Soufflé Omelette   Serves 1–2

A spectacular omelette for a special occasion. Although savoury fillings are more usual, try it with freshly cooked or canned fruit as an uncommon dessert.

2 eggs, separated
2 teaspoons water
1 teaspoon caster sugar or salt and pepper
$\frac{1}{4}$ oz/7 g butter

Heat the grill. Whisk the egg whites until stiff. Whisk the yolks with water and sugar or season-

ing, and fold into whites. Heat butter in a 7 inch/18 cm omelette pan until sizzling. Pour in the egg and cook until golden underneath. Place under hot grill until cooked and golden on top. Add filling and fold over onto a plate. If it is more convenient, the omelette can be finished in a hot oven (425°F/220°C/Mark 7) for a few minutes, instead of under the grill. Make sure that the pan has an ovenproof handle.

Spanish Omelette   Serves 2–3

This is a tortilla, an economical and substantial family supper dish. Use other cooked vegetables if available.

1 oz/100 g butter or 4 tablespoons olive oil
1 onion, chopped
8–12 oz/225–350 g cooked potatoes, diced
3 eggs
3 teaspoons water
salt and pepper

Heat the grill. Heat the butter or oil in a 7 inch/18 cm omelette pan. Fry the onion until softened, then add the potatoes and cook gently, stirring, until beginning to brown. Whisk the eggs with water, salt and pepper and add them to the pan. Fry until cooked underneath. Grill the top until set. Do not fold a tortilla, serve it flat.

Making & Using Batter

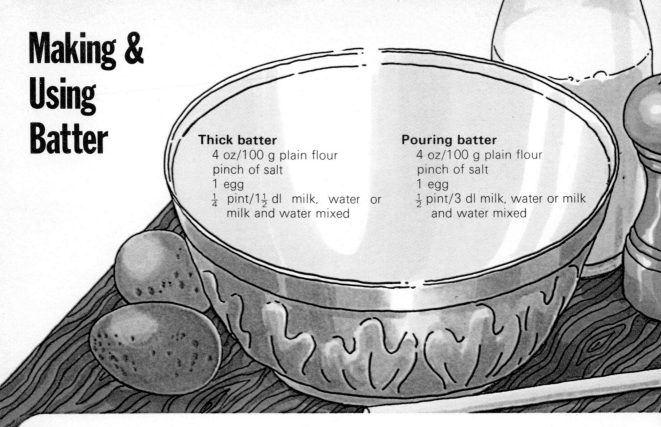

Thick batter
4 oz/100 g plain flour
pinch of salt
1 egg
$\frac{1}{4}$ pint/1$\frac{1}{2}$ dl milk, water or
    milk and water mixed

Pouring batter
4 oz/100 g plain flour
pinch of salt
1 egg
$\frac{1}{2}$ pint/3 dl milk, water or milk
    and water mixed

Batters made with eggs are not only very nutritious but crisp and golden as well (although, as we shall see, it is possible to make a coating batter without eggs). Batters are very versatile; they can be used as a coating for quick-cooking foods and for fritters; they can be made into delicious puffed-up golden puddings, both sweet and savoury; they make light and lacy pancakes.

Freshly cooked batters are crisp — it is only when they are left to stand, even for a very short time, after cooking that they become soft. So serve as soon as possible.

The uncooked batter can, however, be used immediately after making or stored in a cool place until needed.

Make the correct batter for the recipe, using either the thick batter or the pouring batter at the top of this page.

Sift the flour and salt into a mixing bowl. Make a hollow in the flour with a wooden spoon and drop the whole egg straight into it.

Stir the egg into the flour, then gradually add half the liquid, mixing in the flour from around the hollow until a smooth batter is made. Beat well with the wooden spoon. Stir in the remaining liquid.

Using an electric blender
For a very quick batter, place all the ingredients in the blender and mix at high speed for about 20 seconds or until smooth.

Coating batter and fritters
Both sweet and savoury food can be coated in batter, then deep fried until crisp and golden. Slices of tender meat, portions of fish and pieces of fruit are all good cooked in this way. Use the thick batter recipe, or for a more economical but very crisp batter, try omitting the egg and stirring 1 tablespoon oil into the finished batter.

Avoid putting battered food into the frying basket as it will stick to it. Too much food fried at once will also stick together. Make sure that you drain fritters and other fried food very well. Ideally, place it on a piece of absorbent kitchen paper and keep hot while you are cooking the rest.

Prepare the food in the usual way and cut into bite-sized pieces. Trim meat of excess fat and bone. Skin fish and remove bones. Dip the food into plain flour (seasoned for savoury foods) to coat them all over. Make a thick batter. Fill a deep frying pan one-third to half full of oil or lard and heat it to 350°F/180°C. (A $\frac{1}{2}$ in/1 cm cube of bread will brown in about 1 minute.)

Dip the food into the batter, then fry in the hot oil or fat until golden and crisp. The cooking time will depend on the type and size of the food. Make sure that fish and meat are cooked through.

For special occasions when you need an extra light and fluffy coating batter, try separating the eggs and adding the yolks and whites separately. The yolks can be added with the milk as you would when making a conventional batter. Whisk the whites until stiff and fold in just before cooking.

Batter puddings

A pudding made with water only (no milk) will be exceptionally crisp and light. A plain batter pudding (also called Yorkshire pudding) is traditionally served with roast beef.

Heat the oven to 425°F/ 220°C/Mark 7. Make a pouring batter. Put $\frac{1}{2}$ oz/15 g lard or $\frac{1}{2}$ tablespoon oil in a shallow cake tin or roasting pan. Put the tin in the oven for about 10 minutes or until the lard is smoking slightly or the oil very hot. Pour in the batter and return the tin to the oven straight away. Bake for 40 minutes or until well risen, crisp and golden. Individual popovers' can be cooked in patty tins for 20 minutes.

Toad-in-the hole: Put 12 oz/ 350 g sausages in the baking tin and pour the batter over. Bake as for Yorkshire pudding and serve with gravy.

Fruit batter pudding: Stir 8 oz/200 g prepared fresh fruit or 4 oz/100 g dried fruit into the batter before baking. Serve with custard or syrup.

Pancakes
Serve pancakes for any meal — or dessert.

Lemon pancakes: Serve with lemon wedges and sprinkled with caster sugar.

Jam pancakes: Roll the pancake around a tablespoon of jam.

Meaty pancakes: Make a meat sauce from minced meat and a little gravy or condensed soup. Roll the pancakes around this.

Blintz: A Russian pancake. Put 1 tablespoon cottage cheese in the centre of each pancake. Pour over sour cream, sprinkle with finely grated raw onion.

1 Make a pouring batter. Heat a little lard in a 7 inch/ 18 cm frying pan. Pour in enough batter to cover the base of the pan thinly.

2 Tilt the pan to make the batter an even thickness.

3 Cook quickly until the pancake is browned underneath and set on top.

4 Toss the pancake or flip it over with a palette knife. Cook the second side.

Continue making pancakes until all the batter has been used. The amount given in our recipe will make 8 pancakes in a 7 in/ 18 cm pan.

Keep the pancakes hot on an inverted plate over a saucepan of hot water while you are cooking the rest.

Pancakes also freeze well. After cooking, layer them with double greaseproof paper, wrap in foil, then in polythene bag.

Egg Custards

Egg custards are very much underestimated nowadays. They can be made into so many different dishes, some of them ideal for everyday meals, others suitable for the grandest occasions. Custards are basically eggs and milk cooked together, sugar added for sweet dishes as in the recipes given here, or savoury as in Spanish Flan on page 97.

Egg Custard Sauce

This is called 'Crème Anglaise' by the French because the English used to make it very frequently. Custard powder is often used now but the difference is so so great that once you have made a real egg custard you will always make your custard that way, if you have time. Add a few drops of vanilla essence if liked.

    3 eggs
    1 pint/6 dl milk
    1 oz/25 g sugar

Put the eggs and milk in a bowl and whisk them together lightly until well mixed, then strain into the top of a double saucepan or a heatproof bowl. Add the sugar and cook the custard over a saucepan of gently simmering water — the bottom of the saucepan or bowl should not touch the water — stirring frequently with a wooden spoon. You can tell when the custard is cooked because it will coat the back of the spoon.

Baked Egg Custard Serves 4
An ideal dessert for children, invalids and those with a poor appetite, as it is extremely nutritious. Children often prefer a flavoured custard, so try adding one of the following to the recipe below: 2 level teaspoons instant coffee or 1 level tablespoon cocoa; or 2 tablespoons honey instead of the sugar.

    4 eggs
    1 pint/6 dl milk, warmed
    1 oz/25 g caster sugar
    ground nutmeg

Heat the oven to 325°F/170°C/Mark 3. Now proceed as shown in the step-by-step pictures.

1 and **2** Put the eggs and milk into a bowl and beat or whisk lightly together. Do not overwhisk or there will be holes in the cooked custard and it will not be as smooth as it should be.

3 Strain into a lightly greased 1½ pint/9 dl ovenproof dish. Stir in the sugar. Sprinkle with ground nutmeg.

4 Place the dish in a roasting pan with enough warm water to come halfway up the sides of the dish. Bake for 50 or 60 minutes or until cooked and firm. Test it by putting the tip of a knife into the centre — it should come out clean.

Egg Custard Tart Serves 3–4
The pastry case has to be baked blind as for a flan, but do not prick the base as described on page 96 or all the custard will run out. Simply line it with foil or greaseproof paper and fill with baking beans.

 6 oz/150 g shortcrust pastry (made with 6 oz/150 g flour etc. See page 84
 2 eggs
 ½ pint/3 dl milk
 ½ oz/15 g caster sugar
 ground nutmeg

Make the pastry and line an 8-inch/20 cm flan ring, standing on a baking tray. Bake the flan blind (see page 96) in a hot oven (400°F/200°C/Mark 6) for 10 minutes. Whisk the eggs and milk together, strain into the flan case and stir in the sugar. Sprinkle the custard with nutmeg. Bake in a moderately slow oven (325°F/170°C/Mark 3 for 35–40 minutes. Serve hot or cold. Small custard tarts are also very good. Line patty tins with the pastry, bake them blind as for a large tart before adding the custard. Bake for 20–25 minutes.

Crème Caramel Serves 4
A slightly tricky to make but very elegant dessert, suitable for a dinner party.

 6 eggs
 1 pint/6 dl milk
 1 oz/25 g caster sugar
 4 oz/100 g granulated sugar
 4 tablespoons cold water
 1 tablespoon boiling water

Heat oven to 325°F/170°C/Mark 3. Whisk eggs and milk together until mixed, but not frothy. Strain into a jug and stir in the caster sugar. Put the granulated sugar and cold water into a small saucepan. Heat, stirring, until the sugar is dissolved. Continue cooking without stirring until syrup is golden. Stir in boiling water. Pour into individual moulds or one large mould and revolve so that base and sides are evenly coated. Pour in custard and place in a roasting pan with water to come halfway up sides of mould(s). Bake small moulds for 30–40 minutes, a large mould for 50–60 minutes. Unmould before serving either hot or cold.

Meringues and Souffles

When egg whites are whisked, air is incorporated and they become light and fluffy. If the stiffly whisked egg white is cooked, it will harden and trap the air, resulting in a very light and airy dish. Make sure that the bowl and whisk are dry and free from grease or the whites will not whisk up stiffly. Any specks of egg yolk in the whites will have the same result.

Meringues   Makes 16–20 individual meringues
Plain meringues should be white when cooked. For coloured meringues, add a few drops of food colouring. Pipe or spoon the meringue on to rice paper if you prefer — at least you will

not have trouble with them sticking. Sandwich the meringues together with a little whipped cream if liked. If you have coloured your meringues pink, you may like to mix a few raspberries into the cream.

2 egg whites
4 oz/100 g caster sugar
Heat the oven to 200°F/100°C/Mark $\frac{1}{4}$ (or the lowest temperature setting). Put the egg whites in a bowl and whisk well until stiff and standing in peaks. Add half the sugar and whisk until stiff again. Sprinkle the remaining sugar on top and fold in carefully with a tablespoon, being careful not to knock out any air that has been whisked in. Put the meringue in an icing bag

with a large pipe. Pipe small mounds of meringue on a baking tray lined with greased greaseproof paper. Cook the meringues until dry but still white, about 2–3 hours. Cool on a wire rack, then store in an airtight container until required (up to 3–4 weeks).

The egg yolks left over from making meringues can be stored, covered with cold water in the refrigerator for a few days. Use instead of one of the eggs when making an egg custard.

Meringue Nests or Baskets
Make and bake these in the same way as individual meringues. Shape carefully, using a pipe. Serve filled with fruit and cream or ice cream.

Meringue Toppings

Make meringue as before. Spread over pie filling so that it touches the dish or pastry all round, to avoid shrinking during cooking. To serve hot, cook at 325°F/170°C/Mark 3 for 15–20 minutes. To serve cold, cook at 275°F/140°C/Mark 1 about 1 hour.

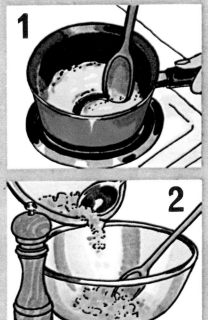

Hot Soufflés

Hot soufflés can be sweet or savoury. They are remarkably simple to make, even though they have a reputation for being tricky. There are two very simple points you should remember to avoid a failed hot soufflé. Use a dish of the right size — too small and the mixture will go over the sides, too large and it will not rise above the edge of the dish. Timing. A hot soufflé waits for no man. Have your guests actually seated at the table when you are ready to serve it. If there is any doubt, cook the soufflé at a slightly lower temperature. The texture will be firmer but the soufflé will not subside so quickly.

A soufflé must be cooked in a dish with straight sides like the one in the photograph.

Hot Cheese Soufflé

Served with a green salad and French bread, this makes the simplest and best light lunch that I know. Choose a well flavoured cheese.

1 oz/25 g butter
1 oz/25 g plain flour
¼ pint/1½ dl milk
salt and cayenne pepper
½ level teaspoon dry mustard
4 egg yolks
5 egg whites
4 oz/100 g cheese, grated

1 Heat the oven to 375°F/190°C/Mark 5. Grease a 6 inch/15 cm soufflé dish. Melt the butter in a saucepan and stir in the flour. Cook gently, stirring, for 2–3 minutes. Remove from heat and blend in milk, salt and cayenne pepper to taste, and mustard. Return to the heat and bring to the boil, stirring all the time.

2 Remove from the heat and beat in the egg yolks one at a time. Stir in the grated cheese.

3 Whisk the egg whites until stiff, then beat a tablespoonful into the cheese mixture (this makes the mixture slightly softer). Fold in the rest with a tablespoon, taking care not to knock out any air. Spoon the mixture gently into the soufflé dish and bake in the preheated oven for about 30 minutes. Serve at once.

This mixture can be baked in individual soufflé dishes, which are attractive when the soufflé is served as a meal starter. They only need to be cooked for about 15 minutes.

21

Cheese

Cheese is a convenience food which is absolutely packed with protein. No other food is so quick to serve but so good for you too. Whether you are preparing for a school packed lunch or for a special party, cheese (just as it is) will be the perfect choice. When you are buying, it can roughly be divided into five categories.

1 The fresh cheeses: These include cream cheese and cottage cheese. Among these two types are so many delicious cheeses from many different countries, such as Demi sel or Gervaise from France, feta cheese from Greece. They can also be flavoured — garlic and herbs are the most popular. The plain varieties are very low in fat, the creamed varieties are richer, and as the term implies, creamier. Fresh cheeses should look moist and appetising, not at all dry or brown.

2 Soft cheeses: There are only two well known cheeses in this category, Brie and Camembert. These are to my mind the ideal table cheeses; I normally just serve a large piece of Brie to complete a dinner party. A Camembert is a small cheese about 6 inches/15 cm in diameter. A Brie is a very much larger 'wheel' which is about the same thickness. Eat the cheese on the day you buy it, when it is at its peak of ripeness. The centre of the cheese should not be chalky but soft and creamy. If the top and bottom crusts actually touch, the cheese is very over-ripe. Buy from a reputable shop.

3 Semi-hard cheeses: This group includes the Cheddars and other English cheeses, Dutch Edam and Gouda, Swiss Gruyère and Emmenthal, besides many others, similar, from other countries. The best way to choose these cheeses is to taste a little first if possible. The colour is very little guide to the quality. Choose cheese which looks fresh and is not 'soapy'.

4 Blue cheese: From the everyday Danish blue cheese to the more expensive Stilton, Gorganzola and Roquefort which are more usually served for special occasions. Taste before buying if possible. The flavours vary from strong and rich to mild and buttery. Buy moist cheese which has no unsavoury brown stains.

5 Hard cheese: These are the strong flavoured cheeses generally used for cooking. Parmesan and Romano from Italy, Sbrinz from Switzerland are good examples. Buy a piece of cheese, not ready grated.

Cooking with Cheese

Most cheeses can be used for cooking but one which is too rich will become stringy very quickly; one which is made from skimmed milk, and is low in fat will be bitty and granular when cooked. If cheese must be heated, never allow it to boil or overheat or it will become hard and stringy.

Cheese slice
Serves 4

This recipe freezes very well and can be served for almost any occasion. Use any cheese available but half Gruyère and half Parmesan will give the most satisfactory result.

8 oz/200 g shortcrust pastry made with 8 oz/200 g flour etc . . . (see page 84)
4 rashers streaky bacon, chopped
2 onions, chopped
1 tablespoon oil
3 tomatoes, skinned and chopped
4 oz/100 g cheese, grated
1 egg, beaten
salt and pepper
pinch of dry mustard
egg for glazing

1 Roll out the pastry and line a 6×8 inch/15×20 cm shallow cake tin or dish. Trim the edges, reserving the pastry.

Danish Blue Cauliflower Cheese
Serves 4

1 medium-sized cauliflower
salt and pepper
4 oz/100 g Danish blue cheese
2 oz/50 g butter
1 onion, grated
1½ oz/40 g plain flour
½ pint/3 dl milk
4 rashers streaky bacon, crisply grilled

Cook the cauliflower whole in boiling salted water for about 20 minutes or until tender. Drain and keep hot, reserving ¼ pint/1½ dl of the cooking liquid. Grate half the cheese, cut the remainder into small cubes, Melt the butter, stir in the onion and cook for 1—2 minutes. Sprinkle in the flour and cook, stirring, for 2 minutes. Remove from the heat, blend in the milk and reserved cooking liquid, bring to the boil stir and cook for 2—3 minutes. Remove from heat, stir in the grated cheese and season to taste. Pour the sauce over the cauliflower. Sprinkle the cubes of cheese and crumbled, grilled bacon on the sauce and grill for 2 minutes. Serve as soon as possible.

2 Fry bacon and onion gently in oil until soft. Remove from heat. Stir in tomatoes, cheese, egg and seasonings. Fill pastry case.

3 Roll out the pastry trimmings and cut into ¼ inch/½ cm strips. Arrange these in lattice fashion over the filling, moistening the ends to stick them to the pastry edge.

4 Brush the pastry with egg. Bake in a moderately hot oven (375°F/190°C/Mark 5) for 25—30 minutes or until golden. Cut into squares or wedges for serving hot or cold.

Fish

Only buy really fresh fish. It should look and smell fresh. The skin or scales must be bright, the gills very red. If the fish looks watery, dull and unappetising, or smells at all bad, do not buy it. Your fishmonger will fillet and skin fish if asked but it is worth knowing how to cope with this yourself.

Preparing and Filleting a 'Round' Fish: mackerel, mullet, herrings, whiting etc.

1 Cut off the fish heads with a sharp knife, just below the gills. If the heads are to be left on, just remove the eyes.

2 Scrape the scales off scaly fish. Use the back of a knife and, holding the fish tail in one hand, scrape the scales downwards to the other end. Cut off the tail and fins with kitchen scissors.

3 Split down the underside of the fish with the scissors. Remove the guts. Wash the fish in cold running water. To cook the fish as it is: Make 2 or 3 cuts in the thickest part on each side of the fish to help to cook it through.

4 To fillet the fish: Open it out, flesh side downward on the work surface. Press firmly with your fist along the length of the backbone. You will feel the backbone coming away from the flesh.

5 Turn the fish over and ease the backbone away from the fish with a knife. The filleted fish can be cooked flat or folded over as unfilleted fish (see step 3).

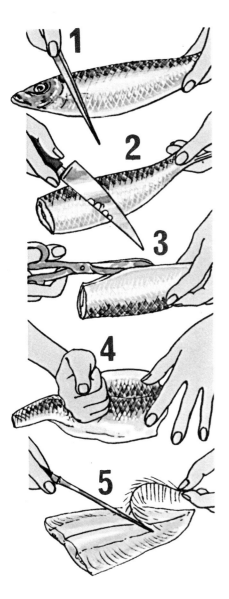

2 Filleting a fish: Using a small sharp knife, make a cut down the length of the backbone.

3 Making long sweeping cuts and keeping the knife as close as possible to the bones, cut away one fillet. Turn the fish round and remove the fillet from the other side. Turn the fish over and remove the remaining fillets in the same way.

4 Skin the fillets if possible. Remove the dark skin; the white skin needs only to be taken off if it is very tough. Place the fillet, skin side down, on the work surface. Using a sharp knife, scrape the flesh away from the skin at the tail end, until there is enough skin to hold on to. Dip your fingers in salt to get a good grip, and hold the skin firmly. Keeping the knife upright and very close to the skin, cut the fillet from the skin with a sawing motion. NOTE: When the fishmonger fillets the fish he removes a double fillet, one from each side of the bone. Cut these fillets lengthways if necessary, for example for paupiettes of sole.

Fish Stock

Fish stock is used for making soup and sauces for fish dishes. It does not keep for more than a day.

    fish bones, skin, head and scraps from 1 fish, plus an extra fish head if the fishmonger will give you one
    1 carrot
    6 cloves
    1 onion
    salt
    6 peppercorns
    bouquet garni (1 bay leaf, 3 parsley stalks, 1 sprig thyme tied together)
    3 pints/1½ litres water

Put the fish bones and scraps into a large saucepan. Cut the carrot in half, stick the cloves into the onion and put into the pan with all the remaining ingredients. Bring to the boil, simmer for 1 hour. Strain.

Preparing and Filleting Flat Fish: sole, plaice, flounder, flathead, leatherjackets, dabs etc.

1 Using a pair of kitchen scissors, cut off the fish head and trim the tail.

Skinning the whole fish: Make a small cut in the dark skin, just above the tail. Ease the skin away from the flesh for about 1 inch/2 cm above the tail. Dip your fingers in salt to get a good grip, then holding the fish firmly on the work surface, pull the skin off in one piece. The white skin only needs to be removed if it is very thick.

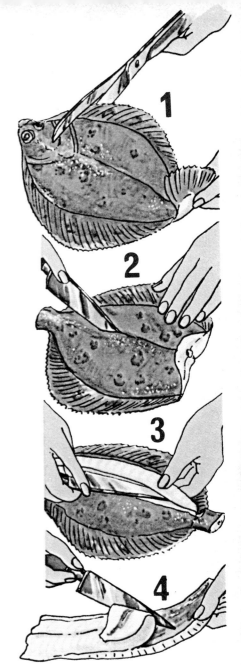

Herring Roes on Toast

Serves 4.

Hard roes are seldom eaten but soft roes are delicious when fried.

    8 oz/225 g soft roes
    1 oz/25 g plain flour
    salt and pepper
    1 oz/25 g butter
    lemon juice
    4 slices hot buttered toast

Toss the roes in seasoned flour. Heat the butter in a frying pan until sizzling. Fry the roes gently for 5–10 minutes or until browned all over. Sprinkle with lemon juice and serve on toast.

Shellfish

With the exception of oysters, which are eaten raw, shellfish are the most indigestible of fish and should therefore be cooked very carefully — and as soon as possible after being caught. For this reason it is usually possible only for those who live near the sea to buy shellfish uncooked. Whenever you buy raw shellfish, buy it still alive if you can; if not, buy from a reputable fishmonger.

Shellfish should be cooked in a court bouillon (see page 29). Do not overcook or it will be tough and tasteless.

Lobster: A raw lobster has a dark greeny-blue shell, but this turns bright red when it is cooked. To cook a live lobster, have ready a large saucepan with boiling court bouillon or salted water. Plunge in the lobster and hold it under the water for 2 minutes. Cook for 20 minutes per lb/½kg.

Crawfish: These are similar to lobster but smaller and the flesh is not so fine. Cook as for lobster.

Note: In Britain a crayfish is a freshwater shellfish. In Australia a crayfish is a salt water fish similar to crawfish.

Scallops: These are bought uncooked, still on the shell if possible. Remove them from the shell for cooking. Poach in a court bouillon or milk for 5–7 minutes. They can also be baked, grilled or fried, but do not overcook. Serve on the shells.

Oysters: Traditionally served uncooked, perhaps with a squeeze of lemon juice. Can also be cooked for about 2 minutes under the grill, sprinkled with chopped crisply grilled bacon.

Prawns and shrimps: These two shellfish are very similar, but vary quite considerably in size. They are normally sold cooked. The smallest, brown shrimps, can be mixed with seasoned melted butter to make potted shrimps. The largest, king prawns or Dublin Bay prawns, are often served deep fried as scampi with lemon or tartar sauce. (For frying see page 28.) Prawns and shrimps make good risottos and salads.

Cockles and clams: Cockles are very small; clams are comparatively large. They can be bought raw or cooked. Choose those with tightly closed shells. To cook them yourself, use a saucepan of boiling court bouillon or salted water. Heat quickly, shaking the pan gently until all the shells are open.

Mussels: These can be bought alive in the shell, even quite a long way inland. The shells should close when tapped; if they don't, throw them away. Scrub them very well and remove any 'beard'. Cook in a large saucepan with 1 inch/2 cm boiling salted water or court bouillon. Cover the pan tightly and heat quickly, shaking the pan frequently. The shells will be opened when cooked.

Winkles and whelks: Wash uncooked fish, then cook them, still in the shells, in a large saucepan with boiling court bouillon or salted water for 15–25 minutes, according to size. When eating, use a pin to scoop the fish out of the shell.

Crab: Choose a medium-sized crab which feels heavy for its size. The flesh should feel firm, not at all watery. A crab must be killed before cooking and to do this, insert a thin skewer just above the mouth; this will go through the spinal cord and kill the crab at once. Cook in boiling court bouillon or salted water for 15 minutes per lb/$\frac{1}{2}$ kg.

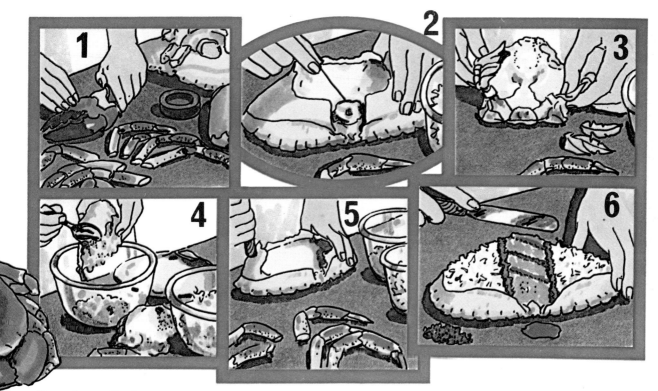

Dressing a Crab

1 Pull off the two large claws, crack them open and remove the white meat. The legs can also be cracked and the meat removed but there is such a small amount that they are normally kept for garnishing.

2 Pick up the crab, shell towards you, and push the body out of the shell with your thumbs. Press it up and away from you. Remove the stomach bag attached to the shell in the head and the mouth which lies just above it.

3 Remove from the shell and throw away the stomach and head. Also discard the feathery gills or 'dead man's fingers' which you will find at either side of the body.

4 Remove the brown meat from the shell and body with a teaspoon. Scoop out the white meat with a skewer.

5 Wash the shell and trim it to a neat shape with a pair of scissors. Dry well.

6 Chop the white meat and season with salt and pepper and a little lemon juice. Add 2 tablespoons fresh breadcrumbs and 1 tablespoon mayonnaise to the brown meat. Arrange the meats in the shell and decorate with chopped parsley, paprika pepper and sieved egg yolk. Serve with a green salad and thinly sliced brown bread and butter.

Fish on its Own

Fish (apart from the ever-popular 'fish and chips') is perhaps the most underestimated food. There are so many different varieties, all of which can be cooked in many different ways. A whole fish, cutlet, steak or fillet, bought very fresh and carefully cooked, makes a dish fit for a king. A perfectly grilled sole and poached fresh salmon are just two examples of how superb fish can be. At the other end of the price range, herrings, mackerel or grey mullet fried in oatmeal, fillets of whiting meunière or white fish deep fried in a crisp golden batter are just as good and make an excellent meal.

Never overcook fish, by whichever method you cook it. It should just flake easily. Here are a few tips which will help you get perfect results.

Grilled Fish: Make sure the grill is very hot before putting the fish under it. Brush the fish with a little oil or melted butter to prevent it becoming dry. The oil or butter can be flavoured with lemon juice, garlic or herbs if you wish to give the fish extra flavour.

Fried Fish: Deep fried fish must be coated in batter or egg and breadcrumbs to protect it from the very hot fat or oil. (For a coating batter, see page 16). Make sure that the fat or oil is hot enough (it should be 350°F/180°C, so that a ½ inch/ 1 cm dice of bread will brown in about 1 minute) before putting in the fish or it may become soggy. Put the pieces of fish in singly or they may stick together. Drain the fish well, on absorbent kitchen paper, and keep it hot while cooking the rest. Serve as soon as possible or the coating will become soft. Fish that is fried in a shallow pan should be cooked quickly in butter or oil. A mixture of the two is ideal; the good flavour of the butter is retained while the oil helps to prevent the butter from over-browning. As for grilling, the butter can be flavoured. Fillets and small fish can be floured instead of coating with batter or egg and breadcrumbs for shallow frying.

Baked Fish: An excellent way to cook fish is to bake it. If the dish is covered in foil the smell of cooking will be kept in the oven. Don't forget to grease the dish or the fish will stick. Baked fish can be stuffed.

Poached Fish: Most fish has a very delicate flavour, and poaching is a good way of keeping all this flavour as well as helping to keep the fish moist. Use milk, milk and water or court bouillon.

Court Bouillon

This recipe can be halved or doubled as required.

4 pints/ 2 litres water
¼ pint/1½ dl wine vinegar
2 onions, sliced
1 carrot, sliced
2 level teaspoons salt
8 black peppercorns
1 bouquet garni (1 bay leaf, few parsley stalks, sprig of thyme tied together)

Put all the ingredients in a large saucepan. Bring to the boil, cover the pan and simmer for about 1 hour. Strain.

Fish Meunière   Serves 4

Any white fish can be used, such as sole, plaice, whiting, flounder, flathead.

8 small fish fillets
seasoned flour
1 egg, beaten
4 oz/100 g butter
1 level tablespoon chopped parsley
1 tablespoon lemon juice

Coat the fish in flour, then in beaten egg. Heat the butter in a large frying pan and fry the fillets for 3–4 minutes, turning once. Place on a serving plate and keep hot. Reheat the butter until it is beginning to brown. Add the parsley and lemon juice and heat until golden. Pour over the fish as a sauce.

Grilled Cheesy Cod Cutlets

Serves 4

4 cod (or other white fish) cutlets
4 oz/100 g cheese, grated
pinch of mustard
salt and pepper
1 egg
2 oz/50 g butter

Remove the bones and shape the cutlets neatly. Mix the cheese, mustard, salt, pepper and egg. Put the butter in the grill pan and place under the hot grill until sizzling. Put the cutlets in the pan and spoon cheese mixture on top of each. Cook for about 10 minutes or until the topping is golden and the fish cooked through. Reduce the heat if top browns too soon.

Fish Niçoise   Serves 4

The fish can be put into a greased dish, covered with greased greaseproof paper or foil and baked in a moderate oven (350°F/180°C/Mark 4) for about 30 minutes if preferred to the method of cooking given. Fillets of sole or other flat fish can be folded in three, then cooked; fish cutlets should be boned. Shellfish, such as mussels or cockles, are also good with this sauce and can be served as a meal starter.

1 lb/½ kg white fish fillets, steaks or cutlets
milk
1 bay leaf
1 tablespoon oil
1 onion, finely chopped
1 clove garlic, crushed
1 (14 oz/397 g) can tomatoes
salt and freshly ground black pepper
1 tablespoon chopped parsley
sliced fried mushrooms and triangles of toast for garnish

Put the fish in a saucepan with milk and salted water almost to cover, add the bay leaf. Bring to the boil, then simmer gently until the fish flakes easily, about 15–20 minutes. Meanwhile, heat the oil in a saucepan and fry the onion until softened. Add the garlic, tomatoes, salt and freshly ground black pepper. Bring to the boil, cover the pan and simmer for about 20 minutes. Stir in the parsley. Drain the fish well and place on a serving dish. Spoon the sauce over the top and garnish with slices of mushrooms and triangles of toast.

Fish Dishes

Fish can be made into a very wide variety of dishes. These are just a few which make very tasty and satisfying meals. Some can be bought ready-made but the homemade ones are much nicer and will save you money if not time.

Fish Cakes Serves 4–6

These can be made the day before you need them if it is more convenient. They make a good family lunch or supper; for more special occasions coat the cakes in beaten egg and breadcrumbs. Use any white fish which is good value.

 1 lb/½ kg white fish steaks
 milk
 1 lb/½ kg potatoes
 1 oz/25 g margarine or butter
 salt and pepper
 1 tablespoon chopped
 parsley
 1 egg, beaten
 plain flour
 oil for shallow frying
 lemon wedges for serving

Poach the fish in a saucepan, with enough milk to cover, for about 15 minutes or until the fish flakes easily. Flake the fish, remove all the skin and bones. Peel the potatoes, cut into pieces and cook in boiling salted water for about 20 minutes or until tender. Drain the potatoes and mash them with the margarine, salt and pepper and parsley. Mix the potato and fish thoroughly together, adding enough egg to bind. Season well. Damp your hands, then divide the fish mixture into 12 pieces and shape each into a small flat cake. Coat each fish cake in flour. Heat ¼–½ inch/½–1 cm oil in a frying pan. Fry the fish cakes until golden, turning once. Drain well on absorbent kitchen paper and serve with wedges of lemon.

Fish Pie Serves 4–6

There are many variations for this fish pie. A shortcrust pastry

Beef

The beef for frying, grilling and roasting will be fine and smooth. The coarser the texture of the lean, the tougher the beef will be. The meat should look moist and preferably be marbled with a little fat. Fat helps the flavour of the beef and keeps it succulent.

The cuts to roast: Sirloin, ribs (rolled or on the bone) and topside. Top rump and brisket should be slow roasted.

The cuts to fry and grill: Rump steak, fillet (found under the sirloin). Top rump (round) and topside make economical frying steaks.

The cuts to boil: Brisket, silverside – both usually salted (corned).

The cuts to stew and casserole: Chuck, blade, skirt and flank. Shin, leg, neck and clod are very inexpensive – they need longer, slower cooking. For a good quality braising steak buy topside or top rump.

Lamb

Buy lamb which is pink in colour, fine grained and moist. The older the lamb, the darker

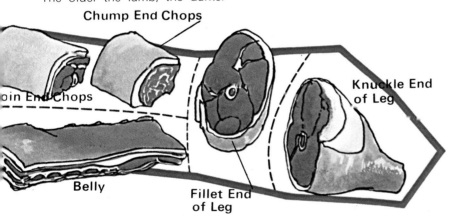

Chump End Chops

Loin End Chops

Belly

Fillet End of Leg

Knuckle End of Leg

the colour and the coarser the meat. The fat should be white and there is normally more of it around the cheaper cuts than the expensive ones. The papery skin over the fat should not feel hard or wrinkled.

The cuts to roast: Leg, loin, best end of neck, shoulder, breast. These joints can also be boned and rolled stuffed if liked.

The cuts to fry and grill: Loin end and chump end chops, best end of neck cutlets, leg steaks (cut from the fillet end of the leg).

The cuts to boil: Boned and rolled shoulder or breast. If mutton is available, this has a good flavour when boiled.

The cuts to stew and casserole: Middle neck, scrag end of neck. Use shoulder for boneless lamb stewing.

Pork

Pork should be pink in colour. The lean should be firm and dry, the fat firm and a creamy white colour. It is the skin which makes the crackling, so ask your butcher to leave it on and score it at intervals.

The cuts to roast: All the cuts of pork can be roasted. The best cuts are leg and loin. For a more economical roast try spare rib, blade, hand and belly. Belly is best stuffed.

The cuts to fry and grill: Loin chops, chump end of loin, spare rib chops and belly rashers. The last two are the more economical buys.

The cuts to boil: Pickled pork is best for boiling. Choose boned and rolled hand or belly of pork. Pickled pork is grey in colour and becomes pink during cooking.

The cuts to stew and casserole: The least expensive is the shank end of the hand. The belly and blade are also good. Make sure that the meat is not too fatty.

Veal

Veal is rather expensive but occasionally you may need to choose some. It should be pale pink, soft and moist – not flabby. There is very little fat and the lean should be very fine in texture. The cuts are: shoulder, breast, loin, ribs, rump, fillet, neck, knuckle, shank, leg (sometimes called topside and silverside). All these can be roasted but as the meat is rather fatless, it needs very frequent basting during cooking. Chops and cutlets can be fried, but avoid grilling unless you use a fair amount of fat for basting. Choose the cheapest cuts you can, such as breast, neck, knuckle and shank for stewing. Butchers sometimes offer pie veal – pieces cut from breast, shoulder, etc.

Bacon

The colour can vary from dark to light red and it should be firm and moist. The fat should be white and firm. The bacon can be smoked or unsmoked (sometimes called 'green'). All the joints can be either boiled or roasted. In order of quality they are: streaky, flank, collar, forehock, gammon. Bacon joints may seem expensive compared with other meats, but most of them are without bone. Rashers for frying or grilling can be streaky or back rashers – long back, top back, short back. Middle cut is also often sold and it includes both the streaky and the short back. Choose a gammon steak for a substantial meal on its own.

Poultry

Nearly all poultry can be bought deep frozen, chilled or fresh. Make sure that fresh poultry is firm fleshed; press the breast bone, which should feel supple. Chicken, turkey and guinea fowl should have a majority of white flesh. Duck and goose have darker flesh. Any bird, unless it is very old, can be roasted, grilled, fried or casseroled. Only old birds, such as boiling fowl, need be boiled to make them tender.

Roasting Meat and Poultry

A roast dinner is enjoyed by everyone but a perfect joint of roast meat is sometimes tricky to cook. It is important to know which joint to buy and the correct oven temperature. Different joints need different treatment, mainly depending on the quality of the meat and whether the joint is a prime cut or an economy cut. The joint of meat should be at room temperature before cooking or it will spit badly in the oven. Heat a little fat in the roasting pan before adding the meat, then baste and roast for the calculated time.
NOTE: For perfect roast potatoes see page 50.

Roast Beef
The beef carcase is large and includes at least seven cuts which are suitable for roasting. The prime cuts are rump, sirloin, fillet and wing rib. These are tender joints which are best roasted at 375°F/190°C/Mark 5. The economy cuts such as rib (on the bone and rolled), top-side, top rump, silverside and bolar blade should be roasted more slowly at 350°F/180°C/Mark 4. They can also be cooked wrapped in foil, after the outside has been browned in hot fat. Serve roast beef with Yorkshire pudding (see page 17) and horseradish sauce (see page 62). Some of us like our beef underdone; some prefer not to have any red meat at all. Vary the cooking time accordingly: underdone, 15 minutes per lb/$\frac{1}{2}$ kg plus 15 minutes over; medium cooked (slightly pink), 20 minutes per lb/$\frac{1}{2}$ kg plus 20 minutes over; well done, 25 minutes per lb/$\frac{1}{2}$ kg plus 25 minutes over.

Roast Veal
All veal can be roasted because the carcase is very young and tender. The meat is very low on fat which makes good eating as long as it does not become dry during cooking — baste frequently. Cook it at 350°F/180°C/Mark 4, allowing 25 minutes per lb/$\frac{1}{2}$ kg plus 25 minutes over. Large boned joints should be cooked for 35 minutes per lb/$\frac{1}{2}$ kg plus 35 minutes. Serve with lemon wedges and bacon rolls.

Roast Lamb
Lamb is a young carcase and most of the joints can be roasted. The prime cuts which have the best and tenderest meat, but of course are the most expensive, are the best end of neck, loin and leg. The economy cuts, which are still very tender although they are cheaper to buy, are shoulder and breast. Roast lamb at 350°F/180°C/Mark 4. If you like your lamb pink in the middle allow 20 minutes per lb/$\frac{1}{2}$ kg plus 20 minutes over. For well-done lamb allow 30 minutes per lb/$\frac{1}{2}$ kg plus 30 minutes over. If you like a crisp skin, sprinkle the lamb with flour before cooking. For a delicious flavour, sprinkle with chopped rosemary. Traditionally, mint sauce should be served with roast lamb (see page 62); or onion sauce (page 59) or red currant jelly.

Roast Pork

Pork is a very tender meat and most joints can be roasted. The prime cuts are the leg and loin. The spare rib and blade or cushion are economical joints but for real economy buy the hand and spring or belly. Pork must always be cooked thoroughly but most people like it with a crispy crackling. Having asked the butcher to score the skin for you, rub it with oil and salt. Put the pork in a very hot oven, 450°F/230°C/Mark 8 for 30 minutes, then reduce the temperature to 350°F/180°C/Mark 4. Allow 30 minutes per lb/½ kg plus 30 minutes over for the total cooking time. Serve with apple sauce or orange sauce (see pages 63 and 64), sage and onion stuffing (see page 46) and a green vegetable.

Roast Bacon

The prime cut, gammon, can be roasted at 350°F/180°C/Mark 4 for 20 minutes to the lb/½ kg plus 20 minutes over. The economy cuts, collar, forehock, streaky and middle cut joints, should be cooked for the same length of time, but boil them for the first half, then remove the rind and roast for the remainder. Serve with pineapple rings.

Roast Poultry

All poultry, with the exception of boiling fowl, can be roasted and this is the best way of cooking birds. Make sure that frozen birds are thoroughly thawed before cooking.

1 Make the appropriate stuffing for turkey, chicken or goose (see page 46). Not only will the bird taste better but also serve more people. If liked, sausage meat or a stuffing can be put in the body of the bird, then a stuffing pushed under the neck flap and skewered into position. Duck and guinea fowl are not usually stuffed.

2 Weigh the bird and calculate the cooking time. Allow 15 minutes per lb/½ kg plus 15 minutes over. Larger birds such as turkey should only be cooked for 10 minutes per lb/½ kg for each lb/½ kg over 14 lb/7 kg. If the flesh of the bird tends to be dry, as it is with turkey, chicken or guinea fowl, place rashers of streaky bacon over the breast. Duck and goose, which are rather fatty, can be pricked all over with a fork before roasting.

3 Bake in a moderately hot oven 375°F/190°C/Mark 5. Serve chicken and turkey with bread sauce (see page 63), cranberry sauce, sausages and bacon rolls. Duck is good with an orange sauce (see page 64). Goose is traditionally served with apple sauce, red cabbage and chestnuts.

Frying and Grilling

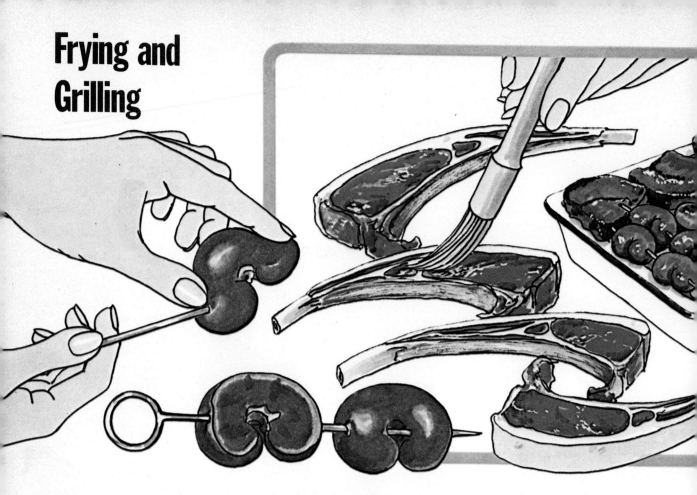

Everyone likes frying and grilling because they are so quick to do. The prime cuts of meat such as fillet steak, lamb cutlets and pork chops are ideally fried or grilled, but cheaper meats such as liver and kidneys are also good. Some cuts which are normally casseroled can be fried after marinating (see page 47). Grilled and fried meat should first be cooked quickly to seal the outside, then the temperature reduced to cook the meat through. Butter has the best flavour for frying but overbrowns very quickly. Use half butter and half oil to help avoid this while keeping the buttery flavour. A clove of garlic (or a bay leaf) fried in the pan until browned, then removed before adding the meat, will give a delicious flavour. Try this too when melting the butter for basting grilled meat. For shallow frying, heat just enough fat or oil to cover the bottom of the pan. Make sure that it is hot. without burning,

before adding the food to the pan.

When deep frying, make sure that the.oil or fat is at the right temperature and that it is deep enough to cover the food. It should be 350°F/180°C (a $\frac{1}{2}$ inch/1 cm cube of bread will brown in about 1 minute). The meat should be cooked through before the outside has overbrowned. The outside of the meat must be protected — usually with egg and breadcrumbs. Add spices or herbs to the crumbs for extra flavour.

Beef Steak

The cuts of beef to choose for these quick methods of cooking are the very best cuts — fillet, tournedos, rump, sirloin and porterhouse. Choose beef which is marbled with firm creamy fat as this adds flavour. The following times are a rough guide to cooking a 1 inch/$2\frac{1}{2}$ cm thick steak to your taste.
Rare: about 8 minutes, including sealing the outside.

Medium cooked: about 8–10 minutes, including sealing the outside.
Well done: 12–15 minutes, including sealing the outside.

Chops and Cutlets

Loin and chump lamb chops, lamb cutlets, pork loin or spare rib chops can all be grilled and fried. Trim away excess fat, and remove the bone for easy eating. Tie boned chops and cutlets into a good shape before cooking. Lamb chops usually take 15–20 minutes, cutlets about 10 minutes, pork chops 20–25 minutes. Lamb cutlets can also be coated in egg and breadcrumbs and deep fried.

Bacon

Cook thin rashers under a hot grill or in a hot frying pan with no extra fat, turning once. Brush gammon steaks with melted butter or oil, then grill for 3–4 minutes each side. Snip the fat at intervals to stop it curling.

4 lamb loin chops
2 lambs' kidneys
melted butter for basting
4 pork sausages
4 oz/100 g button mushrooms
8 oz/225 g lambs' liver sliced
    into 4 pieces
2 tomatoes, cut in half
4 rashers bacon, rinds removed
watercress for garnish

Trim the chops and scrape the ends to leave 1 inch/2 cm clean bone. Remove skin from kidneys, cut in half lengthways and remove white core with scissors. Thread onto a skewer to prevent curling during cooking. Allow 25–30 minutes total cooking time. Put lamb chops on rack in pan about 2 inches/5 cm away from the heat. Baste with melted butter. Cook for 2–3 minutes on each side to seal the outside, basting occasionally. Reduce heat to moderate and add sausages; they will take 15–20 minutes according to size. Put mushrooms in pan to cook in the drippings from the meat above, but they will need turning occasionally. Put the liver on rack with kidneys, tomato halves and bacon. Brush kidneys and tomato very well indeed with melted butter as they become dry very quickly. Cook the kidneys for 3–4 minutes, then turn and brush with more melted butter. Cook for 3–4 minutes or until done — they should still be slightly pink in the centre. The tomatoes do not need turning. As the meat and vegetables are cooked, transfer them to a heated serving plate. Serve as soon as possible, garnished with watercress.

Chicken
Chicken joints or halves of small poussins can be grilled or fried. The meat is very lean, so baste well during grilling. Shallow fry in about $\frac{1}{2}$–1 inch/1–2 cm oil or fat, or coat in egg and breadcrumbs and deep fry. Chicken quarters take 20–25 minutes to cook through. Push a sharp knife into the thickest part — no pink juices should come out.

Barbecues
Food is grilled over charcoal out of doors. For pork spare rib chops allow 12–15 minutes, chicken joints 25–35 minutes, 1 inch/ $2\frac{1}{2}$ cm steaks or lamb chops 12–18 minutes.

Mixed Grill
Serves 4

The secret of cooking a mixed grill successfully is careful timing so that all the items are finished together. Have the grill and pan very hot and the rack greased. Have all the meats trimmed and vegetables prepared beforehand.

Stews and Casseroles

Trim the meat, cutting off excess fat and any gristle. Cut into 1 inch/3 cm cubes and toss gently in seasoned flour until coated. Fry the bacon, onion and carrot in heated dripping until softened and beginning to brown, stirring occasionally. Remove to a casserole. Add the beef and flour to the pan and cook gently, stirring frequently, until the meat is browned all over. Add stock and bring to the boil, stirring and scraping away any flour that has stuck to the bottom of the pan. Taste and adjust seasoning. Add to the casserole and stir to mix in the bacon and vegetables. Cover and cook in a moderately slow oven (325°F/170°C/Mark 3) for about 1½ hours or until the beef is tender.

French Beef Stew   Use olive oil and half red wine, half stock. Add a bouquet garni, a thin strip of orange rind, 1 small can tomatoes, 2 crushed cloves of garlic and 4 oz/100 g button mushrooms to the casserole.

Flemish Stew   Add 2 extra onions. Use half beer and half stock instead of all stock. Add 1 level teaspoon mustard with the seasoning and 1 bouquet garni.

Casseroled Lamb   Serves 6
Scrag end of lamb or middle neck, both very economical stewing cuts, can be cooked on the bone. Allow 3 lb/1½ kg for this recipe. Lamb can be very fatty, so skim any fat off the top carefully before serving.

- 2 lb/1 kg boneless middle neck or shoulder of lamb
- 1 oz/25 g plain flour
- salt and pepper
- 1 onion, chopped
- 1 oz/25 g margarine or 2 tablespoons oil
- 1 pint/6 dl beef stock or water and a beef stock cube

Trim the lamb and remove excess fat. Cut into 1 inch/3 cm cubes and coat with seasoned flour. Fry the onion in heated oil or margarine until softened. Add the meat and cook, stirring, until

The only difference between a stew and a casserole is that a stew is cooked on top of the stove while a casserole is cooked in a casserole dish in the oven. There are countless recipes for stews and casseroles, but many are a variation on a basic theme. Try these simple recipes, ther experiment with the variations when you entertain. All these recipes can also be cooked as stews, i.e. simmered gently on top of the cooker for the same time as for oven cooking.

Casseroled Beef   Serves 6
For really economical family meals, try using shin of beef. The flavour is very rich and beefy but you should increase the cooking time to 3 hours to make sure that it is tender.

- 2 lb/1 kg chuck, blade, flank or skirt steak
- 2 oz/50 g plain flour
- salt and pepper
- 2 rashers streaky bacon chopped
- 1 onion, chopped
- 2 carrots, sliced
- 2 oz/50 g beef dripping or 2 tablespoons oil
- 1 pint/6 dl beef stock or water and a beef stock cube

browned all over. Blend in stock, then bring to the boil. Transfer to a casserole. Cover and cook in a moderately slow oven (325°F/170°C/Mark 3) for 1–1½ hours or until the lamb is tender.

Curried Lamb   Add 1–2 level tablespoons curry powder with the flour. Add 1 crushed clove garlic, a pinch of ground ginger, 1 oz/25 g sultanas and 1 small apple, peeled, cored and diced, to the casserole.

Irish Stew Layer the lamb in the casserole with 2 lb/1 kg peeled and sliced potatoes, finishing with potatoes. Pour in the liquid.

Casseroled Pork   Serves 6

- 2 lb/1 kg boneless spare rib, hand, spring or other lean pork or spare rib chops
- 1 onion, chopped
- 1 oz/25 g margarine or 1 tablespoon oil
- 1½ oz/40 g plain flour
- 1 pint/6 dl white stock or water and chicken stock cube
- salt and pepper

Trim excess fat from the pork and cut into 1 inch/3 cm cubes. Fry the onion in heated oil or margarine until softened. Add the meat and fry until browned all over. Sprinkle the flour over meat and cook, stirring, until browned. Blend in stock, then bring to the boil, stirring all the time. Taste and adjust seasoning. Transfer to a casserole, cover and cook in a moderately slow oven (325°F/170°C/Mark 3) for 1–1½ hours.

Paprika Pork Stir 2 oz/50 g button mushrooms, 2 sticks celery, chopped, and 2 level tablespoons paprika pepper, into the casserole.

Chinese Pork Add 2 level tablespoons each sugar, tomato sauce, vinegar and soy sauce to the casserole. Add 1 small can pineapple pieces and 1 red or green pepper, diced, 20 minutes before end of cooking time.

Casseroled Chicken   Serves 6

- 1 (4 lb/2 kg) chicken
- 2 oz/50 g plain flour
- salt and pepper
- 2 oz/50 g margarine or 2 tablespoons oil
- 1 onion, chopped
- 1 pint/6 dl chicken stock or water and chicken stock cube

Chop the chicken into 6 serving portions. Coat in 1 oz seasoned flour. Fry the chicken pieces in heated oil or margarine until browned all over. Transfer to a casserole. Add onion to pan and fry, scraping the bits off bottom of pan, until softened. Stir in remaining flour and cook, stirring, for 2–3 minutes. Blend in stock. Bring to the boil, stirring all the time. Pour sauce over chicken, cover and cook in a moderately slow oven (325°F/170°C/Mark 3) for 1–1½ hours.

Spanish Chicken
(photographed on front cover) Follow recipe above, but fry 1 crushed clove garlic with the onion. Add 1 (14 oz/397 g) can tomatoes with the stock. Stir in 1 sliced red pepper, 4 tablespoons sherry, and 6 sliced Spanish stuffed green olives, 10 minutes before the cooking is complete. To garnish, scatter another sliced red pepper and 6 extra Spanish stuffed green olives on the top.

Chicken with Mushrooms Add 1 level teaspoon chopped dried rosemary, 4 oz/100 g button mushrooms and ¼ pint/1½ dl white wine to the casserole.

Boiling Meat

Meat of all kinds can be boiled and this is a very good way of tenderising the cheaper, tougher cuts. When cooked carefully it can be very delicious and extremely moist. Many boiled meats are cooled, then pressed overnight and served cold.

Boiled Beef and Dumplings.
Serves 6–8
For a really tasty meal, buy salted or corned beef although fresh is also good. Serve with a parsley sauce (see page 59), made with half milk and half the beef cooking liquid. The suet dumplings complement the meat and make it go further when you have a hungry family to feed!

- 3 lb/1½ kg salt beef
- 2 onions, quartered
- 8 cloves
- 1 bay leaf
- 8 peppercorns
- 1 beef stock cube
- 8 oz/225 g carrots, sliced

Dumplings:
- 4 oz/100 g plain flour
- pinch salt
- 1 level teaspoon baking powder
- 2 oz/50 g shredded suet
- cold water to mix

Tie the beef securely and put into a large bowl. Soak salted meat in cold water for at least 3 hours, overnight if very salty. Put into a deep saucepan with enough cold water to cover. Bring to the boil, then skim. Add the onions stuck with the cloves, bay leaf, peppercorns and stock cube. Cover the saucepan and simmer gently for 2 hours 40 minutes, (allow 40 minutes per lb/½ kg and 40 minutes over). Add the carrots after 1 hour of cooking. Make the dumplings: Sift the flour, salt and baking powder into a mixing bowl. Stir in the suet, then enough cold water to make a soft dough. Shape the dough into small balls about 1 inch/3 cm in diameter. Put the dumplings in the cooking liquid for the last 20 minutes of cooking time. Drain the meat and serve surrounded by dumplings and carrots.

Boiled Bacon

Serves 6–8

Boiled bacon makes a delicious meal served either hot or cold. All bacon joints are good boiled, from the expensive gammon to the cheaper forehock or collar joints. Most bacon joints have only a mild cure nowadays and do not need overnight soaking.

   3 lb/1½ kg boned bacon joint
   1 bay leaf
   6 peppercorns
   1 tablespoon brown sugar
   1 onion
   4 cloves
   browned breadcrumbs

Tie the joint firmly in shape and put into a large saucepan with cold water to cover. Bring to the boil, then drain and add fresh cold water. Add the bay leaf, peppercorns, brown sugar, onion and cloves. Bring to the boil again, then cover the pan and simmer for 1 hour 20 minutes (allow 20 minutes per lb/½ kg plus 20 minutes over). Drain the bacon and peel off the rind – it should come off easily. Press browned breadcrumbs over the fat and serve.

Freezer Note

Meat freezes well either cooked or uncooked. Cooked, check that it is not over-seasoned as the flavour becomes more intense after a time. Try to cover the meat with gravy as this keeps it moist and stops it drying out. If you buy meat in bulk to store, uncooked, in the freezer, make sure that it is good quality. It is worth shopping around until you find a really reliable supplier who understands your needs and will give you good value for money. More and more family butchers are catering for freezer owners today. Pack and freeze the meat in usable quantities. Chops and steaks should be interleaved with waxed paper to prevent them from sticking together. Joints should be individually wrapped. Label each package very clearly as it is extremely difficult to see what is actually inside once the package is frozen.

Spiced Pressed Pork

Serves 6–8

A delicious way of cooking a rather fatty cut of pork.

   3 lb/1½ kg pickled belly of
      pork, boned
   1 onion
   4 cloves
   6 peppercorns
   ½ lemon
   1 bay leaf
   Glaze:
   melted butter
   ground cinnamon

Put the pork in a large bowl with water to cover. Soak for 2–3 hours. Drain. Put into a saucepan with cold water to cover, plus onion stuck with cloves, peppercorns, lemon and bay leaf. Bring to the boil, skim, then cover pan and cook for 1 hour 40 minutes (allow 25 minutes per lb/½ kg plus 25 minutes over). Drain the pork well and pull off skin. Score fat in a diamond pattern. Place the meat in a roasting pan and brush fat with melted butter. Sprinkle with cinnamon. Bake in a hot oven (425°F/220°C/Mark 7) for 15–20 minutes or until browned. Allow to cool completely. Place between two plates with a heavy weight on top. Leave overnight in a cool place, preferably the refrigerator. Serve sliced with salad and pickles.

Minced Meat

Minced meat bought from the butcher is usually beef. If you ask him well in advance, however, and buy a large enough quantity, he will mince any meat you choose — lamb, pork or veal. Mincing meat at home can be a bit of a chore unless you have an electric mixer with a mincing attachment. If you can do your own mincing, however, it is normally better. You can see the meat you are buying, know the quality and amount of fat — but you must allow for some wastage. Sometimes ready minced meat can be of dubious quality — especially if it is sold at a lower price. Minced meat can be made into an enormous variety of dishes. Each country seems to have its national favourite. You will find the Italian version — Spaghetti Bolognese — on page 55 (Pasta and rice).

Shepherd's Pie   Serves 6

Very simple to prepare and a firm favourite in every English home. Add a little curry powder to taste, for a variation. This dish freezes very well ready-prepared. Strictly speaking, Shepherd's Pie is made with lamb — when beef is used it is Cottage Pie.

    1 oz/25 g dripping or 1 table-
        spoon oil
    2 onions, sliced
    1½ lb/675 g minced lamb or
        beef
    2 level tablespoons plain flour
    ¾ pint/4 dl beef stock or water
        and beef stock cube
    salt and pepper
    1 tablespoon tomato purée
    1½ lb/675 g potatoes
    1 oz/25 g butter
    milk
    1 level teaspoon mixed dried
        herbs

Heat the dripping or oil in a saucepan and fry the onions until softened. Add the meat and cook, stirring, until browned all over. Sprinkle in the flour and cook, stirring, for a further 2 minutes. Blend in the stock, then season to taste and stir in the tomato purée. Bring to the boil, cover the pan and simmer for 30 minutes.

Meanwhile peel, chop and cook the potatoes in boiling salted water until tender. Drain well and mash until smooth with the butter and a little milk. Pour the cooked meat into a greased ovenproof dish and spread the potato evenly all over the top, roughing it up with a fork. Sprinkle with the herbs. Bake in a hot oven (425°F/220°C/Mark 7) until the top is golden.

Beefburgers
Serves 6
An all-American invention which has become very popular in this country, especially with children. The homemade variety is much meatier and tastier than the commercially frozen ones, but you can of course freeze them yourself if you wish.

1½ lb/675 g minced beef
4 oz/100 g breadcrumbs
1 onion, grated or finely
   chopped
½ level teaspoon mixed dried
   herbs
salt and pepper
1 egg
oil for frying
6 soft round unsweetened
   buns for serving

Put the beef, breadcrumbs, onion, herbs, salt and pepper and egg into a bowl and mix all together thoroughly. With wet hands shape the mixture into 6 fat cakes. Heat ¼ inch/½ cm oil in a frying pan and cook the beefburgers for about 5 minutes on each side or until cooked through. Cut the buns in half and sandwich a beefburger in each. Serve in the approved fashion, in a paper napkin.

Frikadeller   Serves 6

These small dainty Danish meatballs could be served when you are entertaining, as a meal starter or as a hot party savoury impaled on cocktail sticks, or even for the main course.

1 lb/½ kg minced beef
8 oz/225 g minced pork
1 onion, grated
2 oz/50 g plain flour
½ level teaspoon salt
¼ level teaspoon pepper
½ level teaspoon ground allspice
3 tablespoons evaporated milk
   or cream
1 egg
melted butter
oil for frying
1 (5 fluid oz/142 ml) carton
   soured cream
2 tablespoons chopped
   gherkin

Put the minced beef, minced pork, onion, flour, salt, pepper, ground allspice, milk and egg into a bowl and mix thoroughly. Shape the mixture into small balls, using 2 teaspoons dipped in melted butter. Heat a little oil in a frying pan and fry the meatballs slowly until they are browned all over. Heat the soured cream without boiling. Serve the meatballs with the soured cream poured over the top and sprinkled with chopped gherkin.

Pâté and Offal Dishes

Offal is much underrated, yet it makes wonderful dishes. Most of the tastier pâtés are made from or contain some liver. Ox and lambs' liver, kidneys, heart, all make extremely meaty and economical meals. Veal has offal fit for the grandest occasion, sweetbreads and veal kidneys for instance.

Liver Pâté

This combines the flavours of two livers to make a very good and inexpensive pâté. It is quick and easy to make if you have an electric blender (liquidiser). If you haven't, mince the livers before beating them with the remaining ingredients, but the texture of the pâté will be coarser.

- 12 rashers streaky bacon
- 2 bay leaves
- 6 oz/175 g chicken livers
- 6 oz/175 g pigs' livers
- 1 egg
- 4 tablespoons cream
- 1 clove garlic
- salt and pepper
- 2 teaspoons brandy (optional)

1 Remove the rinds and any bones from the bacon, then stretch the rashers until very thin by spreading them with a knife. Place the bay leaves in the bottom of a 1 lb/½ kg loaf tin, then line the tin with the elongated rashers of bacon, placing them across it as shown in the illustration. There must be enough of the rashers eventually to fold over the top of the pâté.

2 Put the livers in an electric blender with the egg and blend until smooth. Blend in the cream, garlic, salt and pepper and brandy if used. Put the mixture into the bacon-lined tin and fold over the ends of the rashers onto the pâté.

3 Cover the pâté with foil. Put the tin in a roasting pan with enough water to come half-way up the sides of the tin. Cook in a moderately slow oven (325°F/170°C/Mark 3) for 1 hour. Allow to cool in the tin, then chill before serving.

Devilled Kidneys   Serves 4

A quick and easy recipe for lunch or supper. If the kidneys smell strong, soak them in salted water for 1 hour before cooking. Serve on toast or with mashed potatoes and a green salad.

- 1 lb/½ kg lambs' kidneys
- 1 tablespoon tomato purée
- 2 teaspoons Worcestershire sauce
- 1 tablespoon chutney
- 2 teaspoons lemon juice
- pinch of cayenne pepper
- salt and pepper

Cut the kidneys in half length-ways. Skin and snip out the core with scissors. Spread the kidney halves in a grill pan. Mix all the remaining ingredients together and spread over the kidneys. Grill for about 7–10 minutes, turning occasionally.

Liver and Bacon Casserole
Serves 4–6
A very inexpensive and savoury casserole. Soak the liver in milk for 1 hour before using, to mellow the flavour. Serve with mashed potatoes.

- 1½ lb/675 g ox liver, sliced
- seasoned flour
- 1 oz/25 g butter
- 1 large onion, chopped
- salt and pepper
- 1 (14 oz/397 g) can tomatoes
- 2 level tablespoons tomato purée
- 6 rashers back bacon, halved and rolled

Coat the liver in seasoned flour. Heat the butter in a saucepan and fry the onion until softened. Add the liver and fry until browned all over. Put the liver and onion in a casserole and season. Chop the tomatoes and blend the purée with the liquid from the can. Add to the casserole. Cook in a moderately slow oven (325°F/170°C/Mark 3) for 30 minutes. Arrange the bacon rolls on top. Cook for a further 30 minutes.

Stuffings & Marinades

Parsley and Thyme Stuffing
(Veal forcemeat)

This stuffing is best for the more delicately flavoured meats, lamb, veal, chicken and turkey.

- 4 oz/100 g fresh breadcrumbs
- 2 oz/50 g shredded suet
- 2 level tablespoons chopped parsley
- 2 level teaspoons dried thyme
- 1 level teaspoon grated lemon rind
- 1 level teaspoon salt
- $\frac{1}{2}$ level teaspoon pepper
- 1 egg
- milk to mix

Mix all the ingredients, adding enough milk to bind. Use as stuffing or form into balls.

Bacon and Herb Stuffing

This is a full-flavoured stuffing which needs a well flavoured meat. I find it excellent with offal or beef.

- 4 oz/100 g fresh breadcrumbs
- 2 oz/50 g shredded suet
- 2 rashers streaky bacon, chopped
- $\frac{1}{2}$ level tablespoon fresh parsley
- $\frac{1}{2}$ level teaspoon mixed dried herbs
- finely grated rind of $\frac{1}{2}$ lemon
- salt and pepper
- milk to mix

Mix all the ingredients together with enough milk to bind. Use as other stuffings.

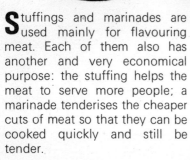

Stuffings and marinades are used mainly for flavouring meat. Each of them also has another and very economical purpose: the stuffing helps the meat to serve more people; a marinade tenderises the cheaper cuts of meat so that they can be cooked quickly and still be tender.

Sage and Onion Stuffing

Use this stuffing for pork, duck or goose.

- 4 onions, chopped
- 2 level teaspoons dried sage
- 4 oz/100 g fresh breadcrumbs
- 1 level teaspoon salt
- $\frac{1}{2}$ level teaspoon pepper
- 1 oz/25 g melted butter

Cook the chopped onion in a little boiling water for 5 minutes. Drain. Mix the onion with all the other ingredients. Stuff the meat or poultry with the mixture or shape it into small balls and cook around the roasting joint or bird.

Yoghourt Marinade

Soak less expensive cuts such as middle neck chops or strips of breast of lamb, skirt, topside or top rump steak in this overnight to tenderise before grilling. Cut into cubes, then thread onto skewers for kebabs.

    1 (5 fluid oz/142 ml) carton natural yoghourt
    1 small onion, grated
    1 level tablespoon curry powder
    1 clove garlic, crushed
    pinch each of ground ginger and ground nutmeg
    1 tablespoon oil
    1 tablespoon lemon juice
    salt and pepper

Mix all the ingredients together. Place the meat in a shallow dish and pour the marinade over. Stir frequently while marinating.

Herbed Marinade

A marinade made with mixed dried herbs is suitable for frying steak – top rump (round), topside, rib eye steak. Use rosemary or mint to make a marinade for lamb cutlets. Not so much to tenderise as to give a delicate flavour to pork, substitute rosemary or sage for mixed herbs.

    5 tablespoons wine vinegar
    5 tablespoons olive oil
    1 clove garlic, crushed
    1–2 level teaspoons dried herbs
    salt and pepper

Mix all the ingredients together. Pour over the meat in a non-metal dish and leave as long as possible, stirring occasionally. The meat should lie as flat as possible but it need not be submerged in the marinade.

Barbecue Marinade

Quite often less expensive cuts of meat are used for barbecues. Marinate them in this marinade, baste frequently while cooking and serve any leftover with the meat as a sauce

    $\frac{1}{2}$ pint/3 dl tomato juice
    1 tablespoon Worcestershire sauce
    2 level tablespoons soft brown sugar
    2 tablespoons olive oil
    1 onion, chopped
    1 clove garlic, crushed
    salt and pepper

Whisk all the ingredients together well and pour over the meat. Stir or turn the meat over frequently. Leave overnight if possible.

Buying and cooking fresh vegetables

The best way to make sure of fresh vegetables is to grow your own. Otherwise, choose a reputable greengrocer and buy vegetables which are in season. Imported and greenhouse produce can have a very disappointing flavour and may be expensive. Even the best vegetables can be ruined by bad cooking — greens in particular. As a general rule, they should be cooked until they are just tender but still crisp — it is better to undercook rather than overcook them. Use the minimum of boiling salted water to avoid making the vegetables soggy.

Asparagus: Buy tight heads; make sure it is not running to seed. Wash carefully, trim any woody stem and tie in bundles of 6 or 8. Cook in boiling salted water for about 20 minutes. Serve with butter or a creamy sauce.

Aubergines (Egg plant): Make sure they are not spongy. The flesh can be bitter, so sprinkle with salt and put aside for 30 minutes. Rinse off excess salt, drain and pat dry before cooking. Stuff halves and bake; or slice and fry in butter or olive oil.

Broad beans: Young beans can be cooked in the pods. Remove older beans from the pods — buy about twice the weight of beans

that you require. Cook in boiling salted water for 10–20 minutes (according to age). Serve with a parsley sauce.

French or runner beans: Avoid large beans as they may be stringy. String and slice if large, otherwise leave whole. Cook in boiling salted water for 10–15 minutes.

Broccoli: Wash and trim stems. Divide into flowerets or leave the heads whole. Cook in boiling salted water for 7–20 minutes, according to size and age.

Brussels sprouts: Remove any discoloured outer leaves, make a cut in the stem. Cook in boiling salted water for 10–20 minutes, according to size.

Cabbage: Remove stalk and any hard ribs. Cut in quarters or shred, then cook in boiling salted water for 7–15 minutes. Also can be shredded for coleslaw. Sprinkle red cabbage with a little vinegar after cooking to restore the colour.

Cauliflower: Trim excess leaves and divide into flowerets or cook whole. Soak in salted water for 15 minutes to clean. Cook in

Kohl rabi: Prepare the tops as for cabbage; the roots as for turnip.

Leeks: Choose small leeks. Cut off the root and any tough outer leaves. Wash very well, cook in boiling salted water, whole or cut in half, for 20–30 minutes.

Marrow (vegetable): Peel, remove seeds and cut into pieces. Cook in very little boiling salted water, for 10–15 minutes. Whole marrow or rings can be stuffed.

Onions: Use chopped as a flavouring. Sliced rings can be fried in oil. Whole onions can be cooked in boiling water for $1-1\frac{1}{2}$ hours. Can also be stuffed and baked.

Peas: Remove from pods. Cook in boiling salted water for about 10 minutes.

Peppers (capsicums): mainly used as a flavouring but can be stuffed and baked.

Spinach: Wash very well and remove large centre leaf veins. Cook with very little water, sprinkled with salt and tightly covered, for about 10 minutes. Chop and drain well.

Spring greens: Cook as for cabbage.

boiling salted water with a little lemon juice added; for flowerets 10–15 minutes, whole 25–35 minutes.

Courgettes (Zucchini): Wipe, do not peel. Cook whole or sliced in boiling salted water for 5–10 minutes (sliced), 20–30 minutes (whole). Slices can also be fried in butter.

Kale: Buy and cook as cabbage.

Sweetcorn: Remove the husk and silk. Corn can be scraped off the cob. Cook in boiling salted water for 10 minutes.

Swiss chard: Wash well, remove the centre veins and cook separately. Cook the leaves as for spinach. The centre veins can be cooked in boiling salted water for 15–20 minutes and served as for asparagus.

Stuffed Peppers   Serves 6.

This stuffing can also be used for courgettes, aubergines, onions, whole cabbage or cabbage leaves.

- 6 red or green peppers
- 1 tablespoon oil (olive oil for the best flavour)
- 1 onion, chopped
- 6 oz/175 g cooked rice (about 2 oz/50 g uncooked)
- 4 oz/100 g mushrooms, diced or minced
- 6 oz/175 g cooked meat, diced or minced
- salt and pepper
- 1 oz/25 g fresh breadcrumbs
- 2 oz/50 g cheese, grated
- 1 oz/25 g margarine
- parsley for garnish

1 Slice the tops off the peppers and remove the seeds and membranes. Cook the peppers in boiling salted water to cover for 2–3 minutes. Drain.

2 Heat the oil in a saucepan and fry the onion until soft. Add the rice, mushrooms, meat and salt and pepper. Place the peppers in an ovenproof dish and divide the stuffing equally between them.

3 Mix the breadcrumbs and cheese together and cover each pepper with some of the mixture. Dot with pieces of margarine. Cover the dish loosely with foil and cook in a moderate oven (350°F/180°C Mark 4) for 45 minutes–1 hour. Garnish with parsley and serve — either as an accompaniment, a starter or a light meal.

Ratatouille   Serves 6

This is a vegetable stew. The vegetables are cooked very gently in olive oil to make a delicious vegetarian lunch or supper. It can also be served as an accompaniment. The flavour mellows with keeping, so it can be made the day before and re-heated. It also freezes very well indeed.

- 2 aubergines (eggplants), sliced
- salt and pepper
- $\frac{1}{4}$ pint/1$\frac{1}{2}$ dl olive oil
- 3 onions, sliced
- 2 cloves garlic, crushed
- 3 red or green peppers, thinly sliced
- 4 courgettes (zucchini), sliced
- 6 tomatoes, skinned and sliced

Place the aubergine slices in layers in a colander and sprinkle each layer with salt. Put a plate on top to press the aubergines lightly, leave for 30 minutes. Rinse off the salt and drain the aubergines well. Heat the olive oil in a saucepan and fry the onions until soft but not browned. Add the garlic, peppers, courgettes and tomatoes with the prepared aubergines. Cover the saucepan and cook very gently for about 1$\frac{1}{2}$ hours. Stir and season well. Serve hot.

Root Vegetables

Root vegetables are very good value for money. They are in the shops all the year but are at their best and sweetest when freshly dug in the spring. Towards the end of the winter they become coarser and are frequently blemished and need to be trimmed more carefully.

Carrots: Scrape young carrots, trim at each end, and cook whole. Old carrots should be peeled, then sliced or diced. Cook in boiling salted water for 15–30 minutes according to age and size.

Jerusalem artichokes: Choose even-shaped artichokes for ease of preparation. Peel or scrape, then cook in boiling salted water to cover for about 20 minutes. Can also be roasted in the same way as potatoes but need no par-boiling.

Onions: See page 48.

Parsnips: Peel and slice, or leave whole if small. Trim both ends. Cook in boiling salted water for 15–30 minutes, according to the size and age. Can also be roasted in the same way as potatoes but need no par-boiling.

Pumpkin: Cut into chunks, remove the seeds and peel. Cook in boiling salted water for 30–40 minutes according to size. Can also be roasted like potatoes.

Swedes: Peel and cut into chunks. Cook in boiling salted water for about 30 minutes.

Turnips: Small turnips can be peeled and left whole, large ones cut into pieces. Cook in boiling salted water for about 20–30 minutes according to age and size.

Potatoes: From the dainty and delicious new potatoes available in the spring, to the big old ones later in the year, potatoes are always good value for money. To boil new ones, put them into boiling salted water with a sprig of mint; cut old ones into equal-sized pieces, put into cold salted water, and bring to the boil. They will take about 20–25 minutes to cook. Old potatoes are best for roasting; par-boil for 10 minutes then toss in oil or melted lard or dripping before arranging them around the roast meat. They take about 1 hour to become a crisp golden brown.

squeeze gently to open it. Put 1 oz/25 g butter or 1 tablespoon soured cream in each cross. Sprinkle with chopped parsley for garnish.

Duchesse Potatoes

Serve these for special occasions — they are absolutely delicious. They can also be piped into potato 'nests' which can be filled after baking with other vegetables or even meat or fish folded into a creamy sauce.

    1 lb/½ kg old potatoes
    1 oz/25 g butter
    2 egg yolks
    pinch of ground nutmeg
    salt and pepper
    melted butter

Boil the potatoes in salted water until tender. Drain well, then mash with the butter, egg yolks, nutmeg, salt and pepper. The potato must be very smooth; if in doubt, sieve it. Put it into a piping bag with a large star pipe. Pipe the potato in pyramids on a well greased baking tray. Brush with melted butter and bake in a hot oven (425°F/220°C/Mark 7) for 10–15 minutes.

Casseroled Potatoes

This is an excellent way to cook potatoes when the whole meal is being cooked in the oven. If you use an automatic timer, brush the potatoes well with melted butter to prevent discolouration.

    1½ lb/¾ kg potatoes
    salt and pepper
    1 level tablespoon chopped
      parsley
    ¾–1 pint/4½–6 dl chicken stock
      or water and chicken stock
      cube
    1 oz/25 g butter

Peel and slice the potatoes into ¼ inch/½ cm slices. Layer the potato slices in a well-greased oven-proof dish. Season each layer with salt and pepper and sprinkle with parsley. Pour in enough stock almost to cover the potato. Dot the top with pieces of the butter. Bake in a moderately slow oven (325°F/170°C/Mark 3) for about 1¼ hours or until tender and brown.

Baked Potatoes in their Jackets
Serves 4

There is no nicer way to cook potatoes as an accompaniment than to bake them in their jackets, thus preserving all the goodness that lies next to the skin. For a substantial lunch or supper dish, they can be scooped out of their skins and mixed with grated cheese, cottage cheese, diced cooked meat or flaked cooked fish (smoked fish is good) as available. Pile back into the skins, cover with foil and reheat.

    4 large old potatoes
    4 oz/100 g butter or 4 table-
      spoons soured cream
    chopped parsley to garnish

Choose unblemished potatoes. Scrub them well. Dry and place on the oven shelf. The cooking time will vary according to the size of the potatoes but 1–1½ hours at 400°F/200°C/Mark 6 is usually enough. A skewer pushed through large potatoes helps them to cook more quickly. When cooked they will feel soft if lightly pressed. Cut a large cross on top of each, then

Salad Vegetables

Salad vegetables should be as fresh as possible. The ideal is to grow them yourself and pick them just before they are needed. Prepare the vegetables just before using — except lettuce and endive which can be washed, dried, put in a polythene bag and crisped in the bottom of the refrigerator.

Beetroot: Usually sold ready cooked. To cook it yourself, wash carefully and trim at top and root, place in a pan of boiling salted water, adding lemon juice or vinegar (1 tablespoon to 1 quart water) to fix the colour. Cover and simmer gently for $\frac{1}{2}$–2 hours according to age and size. Plunge into cold water. Avoid breaking the skin during cooking or the colour will 'bleed'.
Celery: Trim the root and leaf. Scrub very thoroughly and serve raw. Or cut up and cook in boiling salted water for 15–20 minutes and serve hot with white sauce.
Cucumber: Usually sliced or diced (peeled or not as you prefer) and served raw. For an interesting hot vegetable, peel it, cut into chunks and cook in boiling salted water for about 10 minutes.
Endive: Looks like a curly lettuce. Prepare in the same way.
Globe artichokes: Choose small tight artichokes. To prepare, remove the coarse outer leaves and trim the tops off the remaining leaves with scissors. Trim the stalk if necessary. Cook in boiling salted water with a little lemon juice added for about 25–30 minutes. Cool and chill. Serve as an appetiser with a creamy sauce or French dressing.
Lettuce: Remove coarse, discoloured outer leaves. Can be cooked in a very little water and butter in a tightly covered pan for about 5 minutes.
Radishes: Wash well and trim at each end. Serve raw.
Tomatoes: Wipe with a damp cloth. Serve whole, halved, quartered or sliced. Best when raw but can also be fried, grilled or baked.

French Salad Dressing

This simple dressing can be used for any number of salads.

3 tablespoons olive oil
1 tablespoon wine vinegar
½ level teaspoon each salt and French mustard
pinch each caster sugar and freshly ground black pepper

Put all the ingredients in a screw-top jar and shake until the dressing is thick and creamy. Use at once.

Potato Salad   Serves 4

Use either new or old potatoes. Cook small new potatoes whole, unpealed. For home-made mayonnaise see page 61.

1 lb/½ kg potatoes
1 quantity French salad dressing or mayonnaise
2 sticks celery, chopped
1 level tablespoon each chopped onion and chopped parsley

Cook the potatoes, cool, then cut into large cubes. Put the salad dressing or mayonnaise in a bowl, and toss the potato in it while still warm. Stir in the celery, onion and parsley. Put aside until cold.

Coleslaw

A good winter salad when cabbage is readily available and green salad vegetables scarce and expensive. For homemade mayonnaise see page 61.

1 small or ½ medium sized firm white cabbage
1 carrot, coarsely grated
1 onion, coarsely grated
2 sticks celery, chopped
1 tablespoon raisins
1 quantity French salad dressing or mayonnaise

Shred the cabbage as finely as possible with a sharp knife. Put into a large bowl, add all other ingredients and toss lightly and thoroughly together.

French Bean or Tomato Vinaigrette   Serves 4

A quick-to-prepare salad which makes a good summer starter.

1 lb/½ kg French beans or tomatoes
1 quantity French salad dressing
1 teaspoon each chopped gherkin, parsley and finely chopped onion

Cook the beans in boiling salted water for about 10 minutes or until tender but still crisp. Drain and cool. Skin the tomatoes and slice thinly. Put all the ingredients into a mixing bowl and toss lightly together. Serve chilled.

Beetroot Salad   Serves 4

A good winter salad.

1 lb/½ kg cooked beetroot
1 quantity French salad dressing
1 oz/25 g soft brown sugar

Peel and dice or slice the beetroot. Toss all the ingredients together in a bowl.

Mushroom Salad   Serves 4

Easy to prepare and ideal for a buffet or other party.

8 oz/225 g mushrooms
1 quantity French salad dressing
1 level tablespoon chopped parsley

Wipe and slice the mushrooms. Toss ingredients together in a bowl. Put aside for 12–24 hours, stirring occasionally.

Salade Niçoise   Serves 4

This delicious combination of flavours and textures makes a good accompaniment to a summer meal. It can also be served as a light lunch on its own with crusty French bread.

3 tomatoes, skinned and quartered
½ cucumber, sliced
8 oz/225 g French beans, cooked and cut into 1½ inch/4 cm lengths
1 small green pepper, thinly sliced
1 small onion, finely chopped
1 lettuce, torn into bite-sized pieces
1 clove garlic, crushed
1 quantity French salad dressing
1 (6 oz/170 g) can tuna, drained and flaked
1 small can anchovy fillets
2 oz/50 g Spanish stuffed green olives, sliced
2 hard-boiled eggs, halved

Put the tomatoes, cucumber, beans, green pepper and onion into a bowl. Arrange the prepared lettuce in a salad bowl. Make the dressing and add the garlic to it. Add the dressing to the vegetables and toss lightly but thoroughly. Place the vegetables and tuna on the lettuce and combine gently. Arrange the anchovy fillets, Spanish stuffed green olives and hard-boiled eggs on top. Serve at once.

Freezer Notes

Most vegetables can be frozen very successfully (see page 125) but salad vegetables are the exception as they never regain their crispness.

53

Pasta and Rice

Pasta and rice are both imports to our cuisine, but are now widely accepted as versatile and valuable foods. Pasta is manufactured in many different countries although we have mainly borrowed from Italy the many ways of cooking it — it can be boiled, baked, fried and served hot or cold. Noodles are used in Chinese and other Oriental cooking. Rice came originally from Asia but is now also used in Italian and other European cooking, in risotto and paella as well as Indian curry.

Choosing Pasta

Pasta comes in so many different shapes and sizes that the choice is bewildering. However, with the exception of certain dishes such as cannelloni and lasagne, which must be made with the pasta from which they take their names, most dishes can be made with any of the pasta shapes. A Bolognese sauce need not be served only with spaghetti; macaroni cheese can equally well be made with shells or other medium size pasta. For a soup garnish choose one of the smallest shapes. Those illustrated here will help you to identify some of the shapes.

Cooking Pasta

Be careful not to overcook pasta or it becomes gluey and unappetising. Allow 2–3 oz/50–75 g of pasta for each person, as an accompaniment. Use a very large saucepan and at least 6 pints/3½ litres boiling salted water for each 1 lb/½ kg pasta. Add the pasta to the water slowly so that the water never stops boiling. For long pasta such as spaghetti, put one end in the water and coil it round until it is all immersed. Add a tablespoon of oil to the water to prevent sticking. Do not cover the pan. Cook until just tender. Taste it; it should be still slightly firm in the centre. Check the packet for the cooking time, especially for the quick-cooking varieties. As a general guide, however, small soup noodles take 6–10 minutes; medium sized pasta about 10 minutes; long noodles 10–12 minutes, cannelloni and lasagne about 15–20 minutes. Drain very well and toss in a little oil or melted butter to keep the pieces separate.

Bolognese Sauce

This sauce is very popular in Italy as it can be used in so many pasta dishes. For a classic Spaghetti Bolognese, cook 1 lb/½ kg spaghetti (enough for 4–6 people) and serve it with the sauce. A recipe for lasagne, another famous Italian dish, made with the same sauce is given on this page.

2 tablespoons olive oil
1 onion, chopped
1 clove garlic, crushed
1 lb/½ kg minced beef
1 lb/½ kg tomatoes, skinned and coarsely chopped or 1 (14 oz/398 g) can tomatoes
1 level tablespoon tomato purée
bouquet garni (1 bay leaf, sprig of thyme, 2 parsley stalks, tied together)
4 oz/100 g mushrooms, chopped
¼ pint/1½ dl beef stock or water and beef stock cube

Heat the oil in a large saucepan and fry the onion and garlic until softened but not browned. Add the beef and fry, stirring all the time, until browned all over. Add all the remaining ingredients. Bring to the boil, cover the pan and simmer for 45 minutes. Stir occasionally.

Macaroni Cheese   Serves 4

A complete meal in itself, but good served with a green salad.

4 oz/100 g elbow macaroni
Cheese sauce:
  2 oz/50 g butter or margarine
  2 oz/50 g plain flour
  ½ pint/3 dl milk
  6 oz/175 g grated cheese
  ½ level teaspoon made mustard
  salt and pepper
1 tomato, skinned, for garnish

Cook and drain macaroni. Use ½ pint/3 dl cooking water with the milk to make white sauce (page 58). Remove pan from heat and stir in 4 oz/125 g cheese. Add macaroni and stir. Taste and season. Pour into a greased 3 pint/1¾ litre pie dish and sprinkle with remaining cheese. Top with slices of tomato. Bake in a moderately hot oven (375°F/190°C/Mark 5) for 40 minutes or brown under a hot grill.

Lasagne   Serves 4–6

Make this a day in advance if it is more convenient.

4 oz/100 g lasagne, cooked
1 quantity Bolognese sauce
1 pint/6 dl cheese sauce (see macaroni cheese)
2 oz/50 g grated cheese

Arrange layers of Bolognese sauce, cheese sauce and lasagne in a 3 pint/1¾ litre pie dish, finishing with pasta and cheese sauce. Sprinkle with cheese and bake in a moderately hot oven (375°F/190°C/Mark 5) for about 40 minutes or until browned on top.

Rice

There are two main types of rice — long grain and short grain. Short grain is used for sweet milk puddings and is the correct type for Chinese cooking.

Cooking Long Grain Rice

Time the cooking of rice carefully as it becomes very soggy if overcooked. If this happens, try to separate the grains by washing under hot running water.

Method 1: Use a large saucepan with plenty of boiling salted water. Sprinkle in the rice and cook uncovered about 15 minutes or until tender. Drain well.

Method 2: Put 1 cup rice to 2 cups salted water. Bring to the boil, stir once and cover the pan tightly. Simmer gently for 15–20 minutes or until all the liquid is absorbed and rice is tender.

Method 3: Put the rice and boiling water as for Method 2 in an ovenproof dish. Cover with foil and cook in a moderate oven (350°F/180°C/Mark 4) for 40 minutes or until the liquid is absorbed and the rice is tender. Stir with a fork before serving.

Easy to cook rice: Cook as for either Method 1 or 2, using $2\frac{1}{2}$ cups water to each 1 cup rice.

Brown rice: Cook as for Method 1 over minimum heat for 50–60 minutes.

Giving Rice Flavour

Although rice makes a perfect accompaniment on its own, it can also be flavoured.

Onion rice: Heat 1 tablespoon oil in a saucepan and fry a finely chopped onion with 8 oz/225 g long grain rice. Fry until the onion is lightly tinted. Add $\frac{3}{4}$ pint/$4\frac{1}{2}$ dl stock and cook as for Method 2 or 3.

Curry rice: Add curry powder to taste when frying the rice and cook as for onion rice above.

Herbed rice: Cook the rice as Method 1, with a slice of lemon in the water. Add some fresh chopped herbs and a little butter after draining the rice.

Chicken and Rice Salad Ring
Serves 4
A good way to serve rice cold. This dish freezes very well.

- $1\frac{1}{2}$ oz/40 g long grain rice
- 6–8 oz/175–225 g cooked chicken
- 8 oz/225 g mixed cooked vegetables
- 1 small green pepper, diced
- 4 oz/100 g mushrooms, chopped
- $\frac{1}{2}$ level teaspoon curry powder
- 2 tablespoons mayonnaise
- tomato quarters and sprigs of watercress for garnish

1 Cook the rice by Method 1 or 2. Drain well, then rinse in cold water. Remove the chicken from the bones and cut into small pieces. Put the rice, chicken and all remaining ingredients together in a bowl and mix lightly but thoroughly.

2 Spoon the mixture into a ring mould or round tin, pressing down very well. When required, unmould it onto a serving plate and garnish with tomatoes and watercress.

Fry the onion, mushrooms and rice in hot oil, stirring, for 3–5 minutes or until the onion is soft and the rice transparent. Add the stock, bring to the boil and stir once. Cover the pan and cook for 10 minutes. Stir in the remaining ingredients. Cover again and cook for 10 minutes or until the rice is cooked and all liquid absorbed.

Freezer Notes

Do freeze cooked pasta and rice. Undercook them slightly so that they are not overcooked when reheated. Prepared dishes, especially the chicken and rice salad ring, freeze well. Make the basic risotto in bulk, freeze in family sized amounts and add the shellfish or meat, as available, when thawed. All the pasta dishes can also be frozen very successfully.

Risotto　　　　　　　Serves 4

A meal in itself and a good way of using up leftovers.

　　1 small onion, chopped
　　2 oz/50 g mushrooms, sliced
　　8 oz/225 g long grain rice
　　1 oz/25 g oil or margarine
　　$\frac{3}{4}$ pint/$4\frac{1}{2}$ dl chicken stock, or water and chicken stock cube
　　1 small packet frozen mixed vegetables
　　2 tomatoes, skinned and chopped
　　4 oz/100 g shellfish (prawns, mussels, cockles), ham or cold roast meat

Sauces

A good sauce can be the making of a dish and indeed the prestige of the French cuisine rests very largely on its wonderful sauces. It is worthwhile being a little adventurous in your sauce making since it is a very rewarding branch of cookery. A sauce should enhance a dish, adding colour, flavour, a contrast in texture and possibly nutritional value, as, for instance, when based on eggs or milk. Some sauces have the reputation of being temperamental and tricky but, as with all dishes, if you follow a good recipe, you will have no trouble. I am giving you four sets of basic recipes: sauces based on the 'roux' method, that is, thickened with flour; egg-based sauces, including custards and mayonnaise; sweet sauces, based on cornflour; and miscellaneous savoury sauces, including mint, tomato, apple and horseradish sauces.

Savoury Sauces Thickened with Flour

These sauces are made by what is known as the 'roux' method. Flour is stirred into melted fat and cooked to a kind of paste, then liquid is added and the sauce is cooked and stirred until thickened and smooth. The thickness will depend on the amount of flour you use in relation to the liquid. A thin sauce for pouring will need 1 oz/25 g flour for each 1 pint/½ litre liquid; a sauce which will coat the food thickly, such as one served over a hot vegetable, will need 2 oz/50 g flour for each 1 pint/½ litre liquid. Sauces are also used for binding other ingredients together, for example, in a rissole. This type is called a panada and requires 4 oz/100 g flour for each 1 pint/½ litre liquid. I do not like to anticipate a lumpy sauce but if by any bad luck you end up with one, whisk it vigorously with a wire whisk or blend it until smooth in an electric blender.

White Coating Sauce

This is the basis of many other well known sauces.
- 2 oz/50 g butter
- 2 oz/50 g plain flour
- 1 pint/½ litre milk
- salt and pepper

Melt the butter in a saucepan then stir in the flour. Cook the 'roux' gently for 2–3 minutes, stirring all the time. When the 'roux' has been cooked sufficiently it will be granular and look rather like damp sand. (It must not be allowed to brown at all or the finished sauce will not be white.) Remove the pan from the heat and blend the milk in gradually, stirring with a wooden spoon. Return to the heat and bring to the boil, stirring all the time. Boil, stirring, for 2 minutes. Season.

Béchamel Sauce

An elaborate version of white sauce, for special occasions.
    1 pint/½ litre milk
    1 onion
    1 carrot
    4 cloves
    6 peppercorns
    1 bay leaf
    2 oz/50 g butter
    2 oz/50 g plain flour
    salt and pepper
Put the milk in a saucepan with the onion, carrot, cloves, peppercorns and bay leaf. Bring to the boil, then cover the pan and remove from the heat. Leave for 20 minutes, then strain. Use to make white sauce as above.

Cheese or Mornay Sauce

    1 pint/½ litre white or Béchamel sauce
    4 oz/100 g cheese, grated
    ½ level teaspoon dry mustard
Whisk the cheese and mustard into the hot sauce. Reheat but do not boil or the cheese may become tough.

Parsley Sauce

    1 pint/½ litre white or Béchamel sauce
    3 level tablespoons chopped parsley
Make the sauce then whisk in the parsley. This is a good sauce to serve with ham or fish. Use half milk and half stock obtained from cooking the ham or fish.

Brown Coating Sauce or Espagnole Sauce

An Espagnole sauce can be very complicated to make but this simpler version is easier to do at home. Do not hurry, for the long slow cooking extracts the maximum flavour. For family meals, omit the tomatoes, mushroom

stalks and sherry. Food freezer owners can make two or even three times this quantity
    2 oz/50 g beef dripping or margarine
    1 carrot, sliced
    1 onion, sliced
    2 rashers streaky bacon
    2 oz/50 g plain flour
    1 pint/½ litre beef stock or water and beef stock cubes
    1 (14 oz/398 g) can tomatoes
    2 oz/50 g mushroom stalks
    1 bay leaf
    1 level tablespoon tomato purée
    4 tablespoons sherry
    salt and pepper

1 Melt the dripping in a saucepan and fry the carrot, onion and chopped bacon until softened and beginning to brown.

2 Stir in the flour and cook very gently, stirring frequently, until a deep golden brown. This should take some time so as to get an even colour without burning.

3 Remove the pan from the heat and gradually blend

in the stock. Add the tomatoes, mushroom stalks and bay leaf. Bring to the boil and simmer gently for 30 minutes. Strain the sauce, extracting as much liquid from the vegetables as possible. Stir in the tomato purée and sherry; taste and adjust seasoning. Reheat before using.

Onion Sauce

Second only to mint sauce as a classic accompaniment to roast lamb. It is good cold, too.
    2 large onions
    2 tablespoons oil
    1 pint/½ litre brown, white or Espagnole sauce
Chop the onion finely and fry it gently in the oil until softened. Drain. Stir the onion into the sauce.

Savoury Egg-based Sauces

These sauces could also be called 'emulsion' sauces. For thickening they all depend on the blending of egg yolks with butter or oil. They are slightly tricky to make, so be sure that you have plenty of time and patience. The temperature of the sauces is also important — they should be neither very hot nor very cold. All ingredients must be at room temperature before you start. Do not try to freeze these sauces as they tend to separate when thawing.

Hollandaise Sauce

A sauce for special occasions. It is traditionally served with poached or grilled salmon, globe artichokes and asparagus. Try it with other fish and vegetables. Use butter, for no substitute will give the same delicious flavour.

- 3 tablespoons wine or tarragon vinegar
- 1 blade mace
- 8 peppercorns
- 1 bay leaf
- 3 egg yolks
- 4 oz/100 g butter
- salt
- 1 tablespoon lemon juice

Put the vinegar, mace, peppercorns and bay leaf into a small saucepan. Bring to the boil, then boil, uncovered, until the vinegar is reduced to 1 tablespoon. Leave until cool, then strain into a heatproof bowl or top of a double saucepan. Add the egg yolks and place over a saucepan of simmering water. Whisk in a small piece of the butter with a pinch of salt. Whisking all the time, add remaining butter, very small pieces at a time. The sauce will become smooth, creamy and thickened as the butter is added. When thick, stir in the lemon juice. The sauce should be warm and thick enough to hold its shape. If the flavour is too sharp, add more butter.

Béarnaise Sauce

Ideal to serve with grilled meats, especially tournedos of beef and mixed grills, this recipe makes a thick creamy sauce which should be served lukewarm — not hot.

  3 tablespoons wine vinegar
  6 peppercorns
  1 bay leaf
  1 blade mace
  $\frac{1}{2}$ onion, chopped
  2 egg yolks
  3 oz/75 g butter
  $\frac{1}{2}$ level teaspoon meat extract
  1 level teaspoon chopped tarragon, parsley or chervil
  salt and pepper

Put the vinegar, peppercorns, bay leaf, mace and onion into a small saucepan. Bring to the boil, then boil, uncovered, until vinegar is reduced to 1 tablespoon. Cool, then strain into a heatproof bowl or top of a double saucepan. Whisk in egg yolks, then a nut of butter. Place over simmering water. Stir well and gradually add butter in small pieces, stirring well between each addition. When all the butter has been added stir in the meat extract and herbs. Season if necessary.

Mayonnaise

It is well worthwhile making your own mayonnaise. Use olive oil — any other oil has an inferior flavour. This recipe makes a thick creamy mayonnaise. If the mixture curdles, separate another egg and whisk the curdled mayonnaise into the egg yolk, drop by drop, as before.

  1 egg yolk
  $\frac{1}{4}$ level teaspoon each of salt, pepper, dry mustard and caster sugar
  about $\frac{1}{4}$ pint/1$\frac{1}{2}$ dl olive oil
  1 tablespoon wine or tarragon vinegar, or lemon juice

1 Put the egg yolk and seasoning in a small bowl and whisk until well combined. Whisking very well all the time, add half the oil drop by drop until the mayonnaise is smooth and creamy.

2 Add the remaining oil in a slow steady stream, whisking all the time.

3 Whisk in the vinegar or lemon juice.

Tartare Sauce

Make 1 quantity of mayonnaise as above and stir in 1 level tablespoon each chopped gherkins and capers and $\frac{1}{2}$ level teaspoon mixed dried herbs. Serve with white fish or shellfish.

Seafood Cocktail Sauce

Serve 8 oz/225 g mixed shellfish in glasses on a bed of shredded lettuce and coat with this sauce to make a meal starter for 4 people.

  1 quantity mayonnaise
  2 level tablespoons tomato purée
  1 teaspoon Worcestershire sauce
  1 teaspoon lemon juice
  $\frac{1}{4}$ level teaspoon chilli powder
  pinch of caster sugar
  1 tablespoon whipped cream
  salt and pepper

Mix all the ingredients gently but thoroughly together. Taste and adjust seasoning. This attractive pink sauce can also be served with white fish.

Sauces for Main Dishes

There are many sauces which are traditionally served to complement various savoury dishes. Most can be bought ready prepared but they do taste better when freshly made, at home.

Horseradish Sauce

Horseradish has a very pungent smell so plan to make only a little of this sauce at a time. Serve with beef or oily fish such as herring or mackerel.

- 2 level tablespoons finely grated horseradish
- 2 tablespoons vinegar
- $\frac{1}{4}$ level teaspoon each of salt and cayenne pepper
- 1 level teaspoon caster sugar
- 2 tablespoons whipped cream

Put the horseradish, vinegar, salt and cayenne pepper in a bowl and leave for 30 minutes. Drain off excess vinegar, then stir in the sugar and cream.

Mint Sauce

Add a little of the sugar to the mint while chopping it as this makes the job easier. Serve with roast or grilled lamb. It also makes a good marinade for lamb before cooking.

- 4 level tablespoons chopped mint
- 2 oz/50 g soft brown sugar
- $\frac{1}{4}$ pint/$1\frac{1}{2}$ dl cider vinegar

Put the chopped mint into a heatproof bowl. Heat the sugar and vinegar gently in a saucepan, stirring until the sugar is dissolved. Pour the hot vinegar on to the mint and set aside until cold.

Apple Sauce

The sharpness helps to offset the fattiness of rich meats like pork, goose and duck.

1 lb/½ kg cooking apples, peeled, cored and sliced
lemon peel
3 tablespoons water
½ oz/15 g butter
1–2 oz/25–50 g caster sugar

Put the prepared apples in a saucepan with a thin strip of lemon rind and the water. Cover the pan and cook gently until the apple is very soft. Remove the lemon rind and beat the apple until very smooth. Beat in the butter and sugar to taste.

Bread Sauce

A delicately flavoured sauce which is served with poultry.

½ pint/3 dl milk
3 cloves
1 onion, peeled
1 carrot, peeled
4 oz/100 g fresh breadcrumbs
salt and pepper
pinch of ground nutmeg

Put the milk into a saucepan. Add the onion, stuck with the cloves, and carrot. Bring to the boil, then remove the pan from the heat. Cover and leave for 20 minutes, then strain. Stir in the breadcrumbs and seasoning. Reheat carefully if necessary.

Tomato Sauce

This is not a smooth ketchup but a sauce which is part of the meal, not just an accompaniment. Spoon it over meat, fish or eggs, toss pasta in it, use it for an omelette or pancake filling. Use a 14 oz/398 g can tomatoes if preferred.

1 tablespoon olive oil
2 rashers streaky bacon, finely chopped
1 onion, chopped
1 clove garlic, crushed
1 stick celery, chopped
1 bay leaf
1 lb/½ kg tomatoes, skinned and chopped
salt and pepper
pinch of sugar

Heat the oil and fry the bacon until softened. Add the onion and cook for 2–3 minutes. Add all remaining ingredients, cover the pan tightly and cook gently for 30 minutes, stirring occasionally. Remove the bay leaf and serve.

Sweet sauces, with the exception of custard, are not so frequently made as savoury. They do make any dessert or pudding much more delicious. A recipe for egg custard sauce is given on page 18. For a change, try making a cornflour sauce, which is very simple and has many variations. Hot sauces can be served with baked or steamed puddings, cold ones are good with ice cream.

Sweet White Sauce

For a thicker 'coating' sauce use 1½ oz/40 g cornflour. For special occasions, add 1 tablespoon sherry to the sauce; for family meals, add 1 teaspoon vanilla essence. You can use this recipe for a savoury white sauce by substituting pepper and salt for the sugar.

    1 oz/25 g cornflour
    1 pint/½ litre milk
    2 oz/50 g caster sugar

1 Blend the cornflour to a smooth paste with a little of the milk. Pour the rest of the milk into a saucepan and heat it almost to boiling.

2 Pour the milk on to the blended cornflour, stirring all the time. Wash the saucepan quickly in cold water then return the sauce to it.

3 Bring to the boil, stirring all the time, then cook for 2–3 minutes. Stir in the sugar.

Lemon or Orange Sauce

This can be served hot or cold. The orange sauce can be served with duck or pork. For a clear sauce, use ½ level tablespoon arrowroot instead of cornflour.

    ½ oz/15 g cornflour
    finely grated rind of ½ lemon or
        ½ orange
    juice of 1 lemon or 2 oranges
    1–2 oz/25–50 g caster sugar
        or to taste

Put the cornflour and grated

Sweet Sauces

rind in a bowl. Pour the juice into a measuring jug and make it up to $\frac{1}{2}$ pint/3 dl with cold water. Blend the cornflour with a little of the liquid until smooth. Bring the rest of the liquid to the boil. then pour into the blended cornflour, stirring all the time. Return the sauce to the pan, bring to the boil and cook for 2–3 minutes, stirring.

Thick Fruit Sauce

Press canned or cooked fruit through a sieve. Add a little of the juice or cooking syrup to make a soft purée.

    $\frac{1}{2}$ pint/3 dl fruit purée
    1 level teaspoon arrowroot
    2 teaspoons lemon juice
    sugar to taste

Blend a little of the fruit purée with the arrowroot, then stir it into the remaining purée. Put into a saucepan and bring gently to the boil, stirring. Boil for 2–3 minutes. Stir in the lemon juice and sugar if necessary. Serve with sponge puddings, ice cream etc.

Chocolate Sauce

A rich sauce which should be served hot. It is particularly good served over cream buns as profiteroles as shown in the photograph on page 93. For a thinner sauce, add a little milk.

    4 oz/100 g plain dark chocolate
    2 level teaspoons cornflour
    3 tablespoons water
    $\frac{1}{2}$ teaspoon vanilla essence
    1 tablespoon golden syrup

Break the chocolate into a heatproof bowl and place over a saucepan of hot water until melted. Blend the cornflour with the water and bring to the boil, stirring all the time. Stir in the chocolate, vanilla essence and syrup. Reheat without boiling.

Brandy Butter

Traditionally served with Christmas pudding. Pipe in large rosettes on to waxed paper or press into a glass serving dish and sprinkle toasted flaked almonds on top. Chill.

    2 oz/50 g butter
    4 oz/100 g caster sugar
    1 tablespoon brandy

Have the butter very soft, then beat in the caster sugar until creamy. Beat in the brandy.

Cold Desserts

Cold desserts can be the perfect ending to a good meal. They are sometimes rich and creamy, sometimes light and wobbly. There is a recipe for every occasion and most are liked by every-everyone. Many include gelatine, such as the soufflés and mousses, jellies and moulds, which should all be prepared carefully so as to be perfectly set. Home-made ice creams and water ices are so much better than the commercial varieties. Yoghourt, junket and jellies are convenience foods which can be prepared quickly and easily at home and taste much fresher than those you buy. These dishes also have the hidden bonus that they cost less, too.

Mousses and Cold Soufflés

Mousses and soufflés are basically the same mixture, it is the dish in which they are served which gives cold soufflés their name. A mousse can be put in any serving dish, large or individual. Soufflés are set in a specially prepared soufflé dish or individual dishes. You must be sure that you have a dish of the right size; the recipes below need a 1 pint/6 dl dish. If the dish is too large, the mixture will not come above the edge as it should do. Prepare a double strip of greaseproof paper which will go easily around the dish and is wide enough to stand 2 inches/5 cm above the edge of the dish. Grease lightly, then secure the paper around the dish with an elastic band.

Lemon Mousse or Soufflé

Serves 6

  3 eggs, separated
  3 oz/75 g caster sugar
  2 small lemons
  3 level teaspoons gelatine
  $\frac{1}{4}$ pint/1$\frac{1}{2}$ dl whipping cream
  chopped almonds and extra
    whipped cream for decoration

Prepare the soufflé dish if needed. Place the egg yolks in a heat-proof bowl with the caster sugar. Place the bowl over a saucepan of simmering water; the bowl should not actually touch the water. Whisk the egg yolks and sugar together until pale in colour, thick and creamy. Whisk in the juice and finely grated rind of the lemons. Allow to cool. Dissolve the gelatine in 3 tablespoons hot water (see page 70) and stir it into the lemon mixture. Allow the mixture to cool until beginning to set around the edges. Whip the cream until beginning to thicken, then stir it into the setting mixture. Whisk the egg whites until stiff and standing in soft peaks. Fold the egg whites into the lemon mix-

ture gently but thoroughly. Pour the mixture gently into the soufflé dish. Chill until set. Before serving, remove the greaseproof paper collar, easing it away from the set soufflé with the back of a knife. Press chopped nuts around the sides of the soufflé. Decorate the top with rosettes of whipped cream. For an orange flavour use 2 oranges instead of the lemon, plus 1 tablespoon lemon juice.

Raspberry Mousse or Soufflé
Serves 4

Use fresh, canned or frozen fruit. Other fruit (apricots, peaches, strawberries, loganberries or blackberries) can be used instead of raspberries according to taste or season. Make the purée by rubbing the fruit through a sieve or in an electric blender.

3 level teaspoons gelatine
$\frac{1}{4}$ pint/1$\frac{1}{2}$ dl raspberry purée
1 tablespoon lemon juice
2 oz/50 g caster sugar or to taste
$\frac{1}{4}$ pint/1$\frac{1}{2}$ dl whipping cream or evaporated milk
2 egg whites

Prepare the soufflé dish if needed. Dissolve the gelatine in 3 table-spoons hot water (see page 70). Put the raspberry purée in a bowl with the lemon juice and sugar. Stir in the dissolved gelatine. Leave in a cool place until beginning to set around the edges. Whip the cream until beginning to thicken. Whisk the egg whites until standing in soft peaks. Fold in the cream, then the egg whites gently, with a tablespoon. Pour into a soufflé dish, serving dish or individual dishes and leave in the refrigerator or other cool place until set.

Chocolate Orange Mousse or Soufflé
Serves 6

A delicious variation of a very popular dessert.

2 eggs, separated
1 oz/25 g caster sugar
4 oz/100 g plain dark chocolate
few drops vanilla essence
$\frac{1}{2}$ pint/3 dl milk
1 (1 pint/567 ml) orange jelly
$\frac{1}{4}$ pint/1$\frac{1}{2}$ dl whipping cream
crystallised violets for decoration

Mix the egg yolks with the sugar in a mixing bowl. Break the chocolate into a saucepan, add the vanilla essence and milk. Heat gently, whisking, until the chocolate is dissolved. Cool slightly, then whisk into the egg yolks and sugar. Return all to the pan. Cook very gently, stirring, until the mixture coats the back of the spoon. Do not let the mixture boil or it may separate. Put the jelly in a saucepan with 4 tablespoons water. Heat gently, stirring, until dissolved. Stir into the chocolate mixture. Leave in a cool place until beginning to set around the edges. Whip the cream until stiff. Whisk the egg whites until they stand in soft peaks. Fold 1 tablespoon of the cream and the egg whites into the chocolate mixture, gently, with a table-spoon. Rinse a 1$\frac{1}{2}$ pint/9 dl mould in cold water and put in the mousse mixture. Put in a cool place until firm. Unmould before serving. Decorate with the remaining cream and crystallised violets. A soufflé dish could be used instead of the mould.

Dairy Desserts

airy desserts are those which are made from milk and milk products such as cream, cream cheese and cottage cheese. Some of them are ideal quickly-prepared family desserts, others are great for special occasions when you want an impressive dessert which can be made ahead of time.

Family Apricot Trifle
Serves 6

1 packet small sponge cakes
3 tablespoons apricot jam
1 (15 oz/426 g) can apricots
3 tablespoons sherry
$\frac{1}{2}$ pint/3 dl thick custard
$\frac{1}{4}$ pint/1$\frac{1}{2}$ dl whipped cream
glacé cherries, angelica and flaked almonds for decoration

Split each sponge cake in half then spread with jam. Arrange the cakes in a serving dish. Drain the apricots and reserve the syrup. Put the sherry in a measuring jug and make up to $\frac{1}{4}$ pint/1$\frac{1}{2}$ dl with the apricot syrup. Sprinkle this over the sponges. Spread the apricots on top. Make the custard (with custard powder) and, while still hot, pour over the apricots, to cover them completely. Put aside until cold. Spread the whipped cream over the top and decorate with pieces of glacé cherry, angelica and the flaked almonds.

Yoghourt
Serves 4

Homemade yoghourt tastes better than any you buy, and is

also much cheaper. You will have to use a bought carton of natural yoghourt for your first batch; thereafter reserve $\frac{1}{4}$ pint/ $1\frac{1}{2}$ dl of that batch for your next one. Use sterilised or ultra heat treated (UHT) milk for firm yoghourt.

1 pint/6 dl milk
$\frac{1}{4}$ pint/$1\frac{1}{2}$ dl natural yoghourt
1 level tablespoon skimmed milk powder

Put the milk in a saucepan and heat it until just warm. It should be blood heat and not feel hot or cold to your finger. Remove from the heat and stir in the yoghourt and skimmed milk powder. The yoghourt must be kept at this temperature for 8–12 hours until thick and creamy. Either leave in a warm place or, preferably, pour the yoghourt into a wide-necked vacuum flask. Chill before serving.

Heavenly Cheesecake
Serves 6–8
This is a very refreshing and lemony cheesecake.

12 oz/350 g shortbread biscuits
4 oz/100 g butter
$\frac{1}{2}$ level teaspoon ground nutmeg
8 oz/225 g cream cheese
8 oz/225 g caster sugar
3 eggs, separated
4 tablespoons whipped cream
$\frac{1}{2}$ oz/15 g gelatine
juice of 2 large lemons
whipped cream or lemon slices for decoration (optional)

Put the biscuits in a polythene or paper bag and crush them with a rolling pin. Melt the butter and stir in the biscuit crumbs and nutmeg. Press the crumbs evenly around the sides and over the base of a 9 inch/23 cm deep round cake tin with a loose bottom or a spring-form tin. Chill well. Put cream cheese into a heatproof bowl with half the sugar and beat well until smooth. Beat in the egg yolks one at a time. Stir in the cream. Put the bowl over a saucepan of simmering water (the bowl should not actually touch the water) and cook the cream cheese mixture for 10 minutes, stirring frequently. Dissolve the gelatine in 3 tablespoons hot water (see page 70), stir in the lemon juice. Beat gradually into the cream cheese mixture. Put aside until syrupy and beginning to set. Whisk the egg whites until stiff, then gradually beat in the remaining sugar. Fold the egg whites into the cheese mixture. Pour into the crumb crust and chill until firm. Decorate with cream or twisted lemon slices.

Strawberry Syllabub
Serves 6–8
12 oz–1 lb/350 g–$\frac{1}{2}$ kg strawberries
icing sugar
$\frac{1}{2}$ pint/3 dl whipping cream
finely grated rind and juice of 1 orange
$\frac{1}{4}$ pint/$1\frac{1}{2}$ dl white wine
3 oz/75 g caster sugar

Prepare the strawberries, reserve some for decoration then cut into quarters and put into 6 or 8 individual serving dishes. Sprinkle with a little icing sugar. Put remaining ingredients into a bowl and whip all together until thick. Spoon equally over the strawberries. Leave in a cool place for several hours, then decorate and serve.

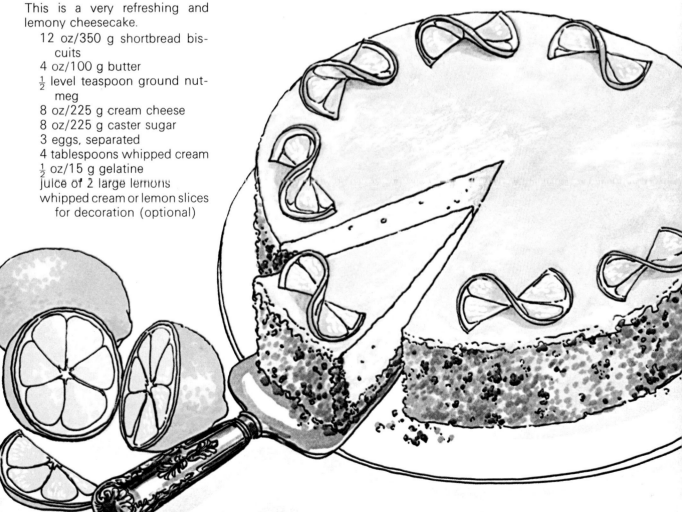

Cold Desserts with Gelatine

Gelatine is used in many cold desserts but some people consider it tricky to manage. Follow these simple directions and you will find that it is not really so difficult. Use a small heatproof bowl or cup and put the gelatine into it with some hot, not boiling, water. Stand the bowl in a saucepan with enough water to come halfway up the sides of the bowl. Heat gently, stirring occasionally, until the gelatine is dissolved. This way the gelatine will be completely dissolved and will never go 'ropy'.

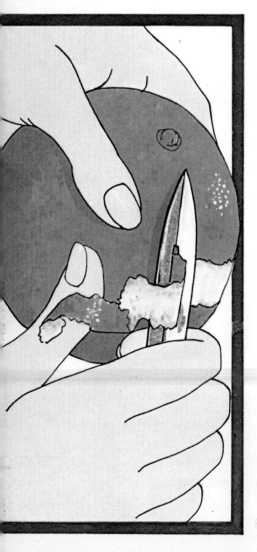

Orange Egg Jelly   Serves 4
This is the best jelly that I have ever tasted. It is also very nutritious, ideal if you have trouble in getting the children to eat eggs. Use lemons instead of oranges for a variation.

    2 oranges
    1 level tablespoon gelatine
    4 oz/100 g granulated sugar
    2 eggs

Wash the oranges very well in warm water. Peel the rinds very thinly with a potato peeler. Cut the fruit in half and squeeze the juice. Measure the juice and make up to 1 pint/6 dl with water. Dissolve the gelatine in 3 tablespoons of the liquid. Put the remainder into a saucepan with the orange peel and sugar. Heat until hot but not boiling and the sugar is dissolved, then pour into a bowl and stir in the dissolved gelatine. Put aside until cool. Whisk the eggs, then strain the orange mixture on to them. Stir until well combined. Rinse a 1½ pint/9 dl mould in cold water and pour in the jelly. Chill until set, unmould before serving.

Honeycomb Mould   Serves 4

A lovely frothy dessert. There are many variations; try flavouring the milk with 2 oz/50 g chocolate or 3 level teaspoons instant coffee before you start. For an orange or lemon mould, add 2 level teaspoons finely grated rind instead of the vanilla essence.

    2 eggs, separated
    2 oz/50 g caster sugar
    1 pint/6 dl milk
    1 level tablespoon gelatine
    few drops vanilla essence

Put the egg yolks and sugar in a heatproof bowl and whisk them together until thick and creamy. Place the bowl over a saucepan of simmering water. Stir in the milk and cook the custard, stirring frequently, until it coats the back of the spoon. Remove from the heat. Dissolve the gelatine in 3 tablespoons hot water. Add the gelatine and vanilla essence to the custard. Whisk the egg whites until stiff and gently fold them into the custard with a tablespoon. Rinse a 2 pint/1¼ litre mould with cold water and pour the honeycomb mould into it. Put aside until set. Unmould before serving.

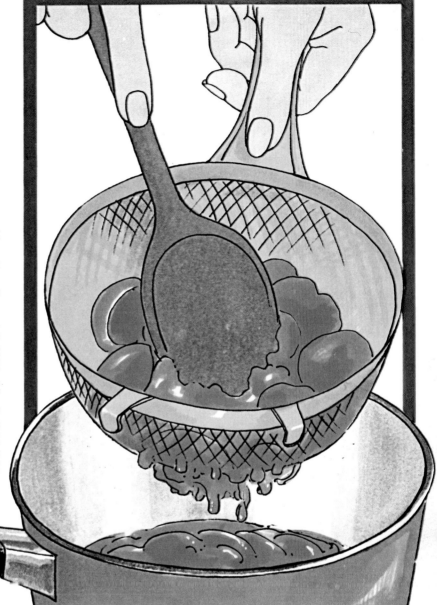

Apricot Orange Flummery
Serves 6

An unconventional recipe which I find particularly popular. It is easier to do if you have an electric mixer. Make the purée from canned apricots.

    1 oz/25 g plain flour
    6 oz/175 g caster sugar
    ¼ pint/1½ dl orange juice
    1 tablespoon lemon juice
    ½ pint/3 dl apricot purée
    1 level tablespoon gelatine
    whipped cream or ice cream
      for serving

Put the flour and caster sugar into a saucepan and blend to a smooth paste with a little of the orange juice. Blend in the remaining orange juice, lemon juice and the purée. Bring to the boil, stirring all the time until thickened and smooth. Remove from the heat. Dissolve the gelatine in 3 tablespoons hot water. Stir the gelatine into the apricot mixture, put aside until cold, then chill until syrupy but not set. Whisk the flummery until very frothy, thick and at least doubled in bulk. Put into a serving dish and chill until set. Serve with whipped cream or ice cream.

Freezer Note:

Cold desserts freeze well and are an excellent standby for entertaining. Dishes which are made with gelatine, for example, the flummery, honeycomb mould, soufflés and mousses are all very good for freezing. Jellies tend to become cloudy, but this does not affect the flavour or set. Yoghourt, cheesecake and, of course, ice cream, all keep very well in a food freezer. The desserts which you should avoid freezing are those made with egg custards — they tend to separate when thawing.

Ice Cream

Home-made ice cream is far better than any you can buy. Not only does it taste better but you know exactly what goes into it. For really easy ice cream making, use real cream or, for economy, evaporated milk. You can freeze the ice cream either in a food freezer or in the freezing compartment of the refrigerator. If using a refrigerator, do not forget to turn it to its coldest setting at least 1 hour before making the ice cream. The freezing should be done as quickly as possible, so use shallow trays.

Quick and Easy Ice Cream
Serves 4–6
The gelatine which is added to this ice cream helps to keep it smooth and free from ice crystals. There is no need to stir it during freezing. Put the can of evaporated milk into the refrigerator to chill overnight as this helps it to whisk up.

   1 level teaspoon gelatine
   ½ large (13 fl oz/369 ml) can
      evaporated milk
   3 oz/75 g icing sugar
   1 teaspoon vanilla essence
Dissolve the gelatine in 3 tablespoons hot water (see page 70). Allow to cool. Whisk the evaporated milk until creamy and thick enough for the whisk to leave a trail. Use a very large bowl as the evaporated milk doubles in volume. Still whisking, add the icing sugar and vanilla essence. Pour into shallow freezer trays and freeze until firm.

Dairy Ice Cream
Serves 4
Use whipping cream or a mixture of half single and half double cream.
   ½ pint/3 dl cream
   4 level tablespoons icing sugar
   1 teaspoon vanilla essence
Whip the cream until it begins to thicken. Stir in the icing sugar and vanilla essence. Pour into shallow freezer trays and freeze until firm around the edges. Put into a bowl and beat until smooth again. Return to the freezer trays and freeze until firm.

Flavourings for Ice Cream
Chocolate ice cream: Dissolve 2 level tablespoons cocoa in a little boiling water. Allow it to become completely cold before adding it to the evaporated milk or cream.
Fruit ice cream: Press 4 oz/100 g soft fruit (strawberries, raspberries, blackberries, currants, apricots etc.) through a sieve or purée them in an electric blender. Stir into the half frozen ice cream, beat until smooth then continue freezing until firm.

Butterscotch Sundae
Serves 4–6
Ice cream is for everyday, but for special occasions try this sundae. Assemble it immediately before serving.
   4 oz/100 g golden syrup
   4 oz/100 g soft brown sugar
   1 oz/25 g butter
   2 tablespoons boiling water
   4 tablespoons evaporated milk
   few drops vanilla essence
   1 quantity home-made ice
      cream
   1 small can fruit, drained
Put the syrup, sugar and butter into a saucepan. Bring to the boil, stirring until the sugar is dissolved. Boil for 3 minutes. Remove the pan from the heat, then stir in the boiling water Cool slightly, then stir in the evaporated milk and vanilla essence. Put a spoonful of ice cream in each of 4 or 6 serving glasses, add a little of the sauce. Divide the fruit between the glasses, then top each equally with the remaining ice cream. Pour over the remaining sauce.

Crumble one of the sponge flan cases into a mixing bowl and mix in the icing sugar, ground almonds, cocoa, brandy and honey. Make the mixture into 1 inch/2 cm balls and roll each one in chocolate vermicelli. Place the remaining sponge flan on a serving plate, spoon or spread the ice cream into it and top with the honey balls. Serve straight away.

Orange Water Ice Serves 4

Water ices are especially refreshing on a hot day or after a heavy dinner.

    3 oranges
    6 oz/175 g granulated sugar
    1 pint/6 dl water
    1 tablespoon lemon juice

Wash the oranges very well, then peel the rind very thinly (using a potato peeler) without any of the pith. Squeeze the juice. Put the rind into a saucepan with the sugar and water. Bring to the boil, stirring, until the sugar is dissolved. Boil for 8 minutes. Remove from the heat and leave until cold. Remove the orange peel and stir in the orange and lemon juice. Pour into freezer trays and freeze until firm.

Honey Ball Flan Serves 6

The honey balls make this a spectacular dessert.

    2 sponge flan cases
    3 oz/75 g icing sugar, sifted
    3 oz/75 g ground almonds
    1 oz/25 g cocoa
    2 tablespoons sherry or brandy
    3 tablespoons honey
    chocolate vermicelli
    1 quantity home-made ice cream

Hot Puddings

Hot puddings are winter puddings. For this reason they are normally quite filling, using ingredients that are available at that time of year. Fresh fruit that stores well, such as apples, pears and oranges are frequently used, as are canned, frozen and dried fruit. Sponge puddings of all kinds, both baked and steamed, make good winter fare and are often served with fruit or sometimes actually cooked with it. Milk puddings are also good for winter meals, especially as they are so nutritious, easy and cheap to prepare and allow of so many variations, making them an ideal sweet course for practically any occasion.

Milky Puddings

Everyone has the ingredients for a hot milk pudding in the store cupboard. The milk can be thickened with many different cereals — rice, flaked rice, ground rice, tapioca, semolina, sago, cornflour and arrowroot. Be careful not to overcook these puddings; they should be soft and creamy.

Baked Rice Pudding Serves 4

A very good-tempered pudding which can be left to cook in a slow oven. It can be cooked under a casserole to make almost a complete meal in the oven. Tapioca can be used instead of rice.

    2 oz/50 g round grain rice
    1 pint/6 dl milk
    thin strip of lemon peel
    1 oz/25 g caster sugar
    ground nutmeg (optional)

Wash the rice well, then drain. Put it into a lightly greased 1½ pint/9 dl ovenproof dish. Pour in the milk, then put aside for 30 minutes to soak. Add the lemon rind and stir in the sugar. Sprinkle a little ground nutmeg on top if liked. Bake in a slow oven (300°F/150°C/Mark 2) for 2–2½ hours. The skin can be stirred into the pudding 2 or 3 times during the first hour of cooking and this makes the pudding creamier.

Fluffy Chocolate Semolina
Serves 4

A light and delicious pudding which is popular with children and is very nourishing as it contains both eggs and milk.

    1 pint/6 dl milk
    2 oz/50 g plain chocolate, grated
    few drops vanilla essence
    1½ oz/40 g semolina
    1 oz/25 g caster sugar
    2 eggs, separated

Heat the milk in a saucepan until hot but not boiling. Add the chocolate and vanilla essence and stir until the chocolate is melted. Sprinkle in the semolina. Bring to the boil, stirring all the time, then reduce the heat and simmer gently, stirring, for 5 minutes. Stir in the sugar. Allow the mixture to cool for 10 minutes, then beat in the egg yolks. Whisk the whites until stiff and fold them into the semolina with a tablespoon. Put the pudding into a lightly greased 2 pint/1¼ litre ovenproof dish. Bake in a moderate oven (350°F/180°C/Mark 4) for 15–20 minutes. Serve immediately.

Bread and Butter Pudding
Serves 4

This good old-fashioned pudding is still a firm favourite with most families. The milk in this case is thickened not with cereals but by a combination of egg and the actual bread and butter.

    6 thin slices bread and butter
    2 oz/50 g mixed dried fruit
    1 oz/25 g sugar
    2 eggs
    1 pint/6 dl milk
    ground nutmeg

Remove the crusts from the slices of bread and cut into quarters. Place half the bread and butter in a greased 2 pint/ 1¼ litre ovenproof dish. Sprinkle with the fruit and half the sugar. Arrange the remaining bread on top, butter side up, and sprinkle with the rest of the sugar. Beat the eggs and milk together, then strain over the bread. Leave for 30 minutes. Sprinkle the top with ground nutmeg and bake in a moderately slow oven (325°F/170°C/Mark 3) for about 45 minutes or until the pudding is set and is crisp and golden on top.

Caramel Vienna Pudding
Serves 4

Although similar to a bread and butter pudding, this one is suitable for the most special occasions. It is ideal served with a sherry-flavoured sweet white sauce (see page 64)

    1 oz/25 g lump sugar
    ½ pint/3 dl milk
    4 oz/100 g white bread
    2 eggs
    1 tablespoon sherry
    2 oz/50 g sultanas
    1 oz/25 g mixed peel
    1 oz/25 g soft brown sugar
    finely grated rind of 1 lemon

Put the lump sugar in a small heavy saucepan with 4 tablespoons water. Bring to the boil, stirring until the sugar is dissolved. Boil, without stirring, until the caramel is golden. Remove the pan from the heat and add the milk. Stir until the caramel is dissolved. Remove the crusts from the bread and cut it into small dice, then put into a bowl. Beat the eggs with the caramel milk and sherry. Strain onto the bread, add all the remaining ingredients and mix well. Set aside for 30 minutes. Put the mixture into a greased 1 pint/6 dl pudding basin and cover with a double thickness of greased greaseproof paper. Place in a pan with 1 inch/3 cm warm water. Bake in a moderately slow oven (325°F/170°C/Mark 3) for about 1½ hours or until firm. Turn the pudding out onto a warmed plate and serve.

Steamed Suet Puddings

Steamed puddings, served piping hot, are ideal for wintry days when the family comes in cold and very hungry. They are surprisingly simple to make if you observe one precaution. With this very moist method of cooking, there is always a danger of the pudding becoming soggy. To avoid this the pudding must either be covered with a double thickness of well greased greaseproof paper, or foil, tied securely under the rim of the bowl with string. If you do not have a steamer, the pudding can be cooked in a large saucepan with enough water to come halfway up the sides of the basin. Stand the basin on a rack or a piece of newspaper to prevent it from cracking. The water must never stop boiling, so if it looks as though it might boil dry, have more boiling water ready for 'topping-up'.

Christmas Pudding Serves 6
This traditional recipe should be served with egg custard sauce (see page 18). It is a very rich fruity pudding.

4 oz/100 g self-raising flour
4 oz/100 g soft white breadcrumbs
4 oz/100 g shredded suet
12 oz/350 g mixed dried fruit (currants, sultanas and raisins)
2 oz/50 g mixed peel, chopped
2 oz/50 g almonds, blanched
4 oz/100 g soft brown sugar
grated rind and juice of 1 lemon
$\frac{1}{2}$ level teaspoon mixed spice
pinch of ground nutmeg
pinch of salt
3 eggs, beaten
about $\frac{1}{2}$ pint/3 dl brown ale or beer

Put all the ingredients in a large mixing bowl and stir until very well mixed. You should have a soft dropping consistency. Grease a 2 pint/1 litre pudding basin and put the mixture into it. Cover with a double thickness of greased greaseproof paper or foil and tie securely. Steam for 6 hours. Either serve straight away or store in the basin for up to one year. To reheat, steam for a further 2 hours.

Jam or Marmalade Suet Pudding
Serves 4

This is a very basic recipe to

orange or lemon flavour by grating the peel into the mixture and using the juice instead of some of the liquid.

4 oz/100 g plain flour
2 level teaspoons baking powder
4 oz/100 g fresh breadcrumbs
4 oz/100 g shredded suet
pinch of salt
4 oz/100 g caster sugar
1 egg
about ¼ pint/1½ dl milk
3 tablespoons jam or marmalade

Sift the flour and baking powder into a bowl. Stir in remaining

basin on to a hot plate and serve with extra jam or marmalade and custard.

Fruit Suet Pudding
Serves 6–8

Apples, rhubarb, plums, gooseberries and indeed most fruit can be used in this pudding. Choose one which is in season, or use frozen or canned fruit.

8 oz/200 g self-raising flour
1 level teaspoon salt
4 oz/100 g shredded suet
cold water to mix
2 lb/1 kg fruit
4 oz/100 g sugar, or to taste

Sift the flour and salt into a mixing bowl, stir in the suet and enough cold water to make a soft dough. Roll out the dough to line a 2 pint/1 litre pudding basin, leaving enough to make a lid (see page 88). Layer the prepared fruit with the sugar, finishing with a layer of fruit. Cover the pudding with a double thickness of greased greaseproof paper or foil with a pleat in the centre to allow the pudding to rise. Tie securely, then steam for 1½ hours. Turn the pudding out of the basin onto a hot plate. Serve with custard.

which you could add many variations. Omitting the jam or marmalade, you can add 4 oz/100 g dried fruit — raisins, sultanas, currants, dates, apricots, prunes, glacé cherries and so on — one or more of these or even nuts can be used. For a coconut pudding, add 2 oz/50 g desiccated coconut. Add an

ingredients except jam to make a soft dropping consistency. Grease a 1½ pint/9 dl pudding basin. Put the jam in the base, then spoon the pudding mixture on top. Cover the basin with a double thickness of greased greaseproof paper or foil and secure with string. Steam for 2–2½ hours. Turn out of the

Sponge Puddings

Sponge puddings which are made by creaming the fat and sugar together, can be steamed or baked. Whichever way you cook them, the preparation is exactly the same.

Coconut Syrup Pudding
Serves 6
This is a very light, melt-in-the mouth steamed pudding. For a special occasion try adding 1 level teaspoon ground ginger or the grated rind of an orange or lemon. The basic pudding can be served with extra golden syrup. If you have added extra flavouring, try serving an orange or lemon sauce (see page 64). The pudding can also be baked in the oven.

2 oz/50 g desiccated coconut
$\frac{1}{4}$ pint/1$\frac{1}{2}$ dl milk
4 oz/100 g golden syrup
4 oz/100 g butter
4 oz/100 g caster sugar
2 eggs, beaten
6 oz/175 g self-raising flour

Put the coconut in a bowl, stir in the milk and leave to soak. Grease a 2 pint/1$\frac{1}{4}$ litre pudding basin and put the syrup into the base of it. Cream the butter and sugar together until light and fluffy. Beat in the eggs gradually, beating well after each addition. Fold in the flour and stir in the soaked coconut. Put the mixture into the pudding basin, cover with greased grease-proof paper or foil (see page 76). Steam for 2–2$\frac{1}{2}$ hours. Turn out and serve. Or bake in an oven-proof pie dish at 350°F/180°C/Mark 4 for 45 minutes to 1 hour. Or cook in six individual moulds (steam for about 1 hour or bake for 30–35 minutes). Individual servings are ideal for storing in the freezer.

Pineapple Lemon Upside Down Pudding   Serves 4

There are many variations to this pudding and a wide variety of fruit can be used instead of the pineapple. Try apricot or plum halves, peach slices, cherries. Pears are particularly good with a gingerbread mixture. Serve with custard or lemon sauce (see page 64).

Topping:
    1 oz/25 g butter
    1 oz/25 g soft brown sugar
    5 pineapple rings
    5 maraschino or glacé cherries
Sponge:
    4 oz/100 g butter
    4 oz/100 g caster sugar
    finely grated rind of 1 lemon
    2 eggs, beaten
    8 oz/225 g self-raising flour
    4 tablespoons milk

Heat the oven to 350°F/180°C/Mark 4. Grease an 8 inch/20 cm shallow round cake tin. Make the topping: Cream the butter and sugar together, then spread over the base of the tin. Arrange the pineapple rings and cherries on top. Make the sponge: Cream the butter and sugar together with the lemon rind until light and fluffy. Add the eggs gradually, beating well after each addition. Sift the flour and fold it into the creamed mixture with the milk. Spread the sponge over the fruit in the cake tin. Bake in the preheated oven for 45 minutes or until well risen and golden. Turn the pudding out of the tin onto a plate and serve hot.

Lemon Delicious Pudding
Serves 4

This baked pudding is a favourite of mine, not only because it is very lemony but it has a built-in sauce underneath when cooked.

    2 oz/50 g butter
    4 oz/100 g caster sugar
    1 teaspoon finely grated lemon
      rind
    2 eggs, separated
    2 oz/50 g self-raising flour
    pinch of salt
    $\frac{1}{4}$ pint/1$\frac{1}{2}$ dl milk
    juice of 2 lemons

Heat the oven to 350°F/180°C/Mark 4. Grease a 1 pint/6 dl pie dish. Cream the butter, sugar and lemon rind together in a mixing bowl. Beat in the egg yolks. Sift the flour and salt together, then fold in with the milk. Stir in the lemon juice. Whisk the egg whites until stiff. Fold the lemon mixture into the egg whites a little at a time. Put the mixture into the pie dish and stand it in a roasting pan with enough cold water to come halfway up the sides of the dish. Bake in the preheated oven for about 45 minutes or until golden. Serve hot.

Freezer tip: Sponge puddings freeze well and it is worthwhile making two or three at a time, eating one and freezing the rest for later. The storage time of suet puddings is limited, however, and it is not advisable to freeze them for longer than 4–6 weeks. Frozen fruit is ideal for hot puddings when fresh is out of season. Keep a supply of crumble mix ready for emergencies. It is not a good idea to freeze milk puddings or those made with an egg custard.

Baked Fruit Puddings

Baked fruit puddings make use of those fruits which are readily available in the winter months. Apples, pears and rhubarb are among the best and cheapest — much more flavoursome than canned or frozen fruit.

Baked Apples   Serves 4
Other dried fruit could be used for filling — raisins, currants, dates, apricots etc.

   4 large cooking apples
   4 level tablespoons golder syrup
   2 oz/50 g sultanas
   finely grated rind of $\frac{1}{2}$ lemon

Wash the apples, remove the cores and score the skins lightly all round. Mix the syrup, sultanas and lemon rind together. Stand the apples in a shallow ovenproof dish and fill the core holes with the fruit mixture. Bake in a moderate oven (350°F/180°C/Mark 4) for about 30 minutes or until the apples are tender. Serve with custard or more syrup.

Fruit Crumble   Serves 4
Fresh fruit, canned fruit or ready prepared canned pie filling could be used with this recipe. If you keep a rubbed-in shortcrust pastry mix (home-made) in the refrigerator, simply weigh out 6 oz/150 g and stir in 2 oz/50 g caster sugar for the topping. Serve the crumble with custard or cream.

Filling:
   $1\frac{1}{2}$ lb/$\frac{3}{4}$ kg apples, rhubarb, gooseberries or other fresh fruit
   about 4 oz/100 g demerara sugar or to taste

Crumble:
   4 oz/100 g plain flour
   2 oz/50 g butter
   2 oz/50 g caster sugar

Heat the oven to 375°F/190°C/Mark 5. Prepare the fruit and slice if large. Layer the fruit and sugar in a lightly greased $1\frac{1}{2}$ pint/9 dl ovenproof dish, finishing with a layer of fruit. Make the crumble: Sift the flour into a mixing bowl, and rub in the butter with your fingertips until the

mixture resembles fine bread-crumbs. Stir in the sugar. Spread the crumble over the fruit. Bake in the preheated oven for 30 minutes or until the crumble is browned and the fruit cooked. Can be served cold.

Rhubarb Charlotte Serves 4
A crispy topped pudding which can be left in the oven to cook under a casserole or roast joint. Gooseberries and apples are also good in this recipe as a change

from rhubarb. Serve with custard or cream.

1 lb/$\frac{1}{2}$ kg rhubarb
3 oz/75 g soft white bread-crumbs
3 oz/75 g demerara sugar
2 tablespoons golden syrup
juice of 1 lemon

Heat the oven to 325°F/170°C/Mark 3. Prepare the rhubarb and cut into $\frac{1}{2}$ inch/1 cm pieces. Grease a $\frac{3}{4}$ pint/4$\frac{1}{2}$ dl pie dish and layer the rhubarb with the breadcrumbs and sugar, finishing with breadcrumbs. The dish will be very full but the filling sinks down during cooking. Heat the syrup with the lemon juice until mixed. Drizzle the syrup evenly over the top of the charlotte. Bake in the preheated oven for 1$\frac{1}{2}$ hours or until the top is golden and the rhubarb cooked. Serve hot.

Eve's Pudding Serves 4
A baked sponge pudding which could be cooked with any fruit you like, but the apple is traditional for Eve's pudding!

Filling:
1 lb/$\frac{1}{2}$ kg cooking apples
3 oz/75 g caster sugar
Sponge:
2 oz/50 g butter
3 oz/75 g caster sugar
finely grated rind of $\frac{1}{2}$ lemon
1 egg
4 oz/100 g self-raising flour
pinch of salt
4 tablespoons milk

Heat the oven to 350°F/180°C/Mark 4. Peel, core and slice the apples. Grease a 2 pint/1$\frac{1}{4}$ litre ovenproof dish. Layer the apple slices with the caster sugar, finishing with apple. Make the sponge: Cream the butter and sugar together with the lemon rind until light and fluffy. Beat in the egg. Sift the flour and salt together, then fold into the creamed mixture with the milk. Spread the sponge over the apple. Bake in the preheated oven for 1–1$\frac{1}{4}$ hours or until the sponge is well risen and golden, and the apple cooked. Serve with custard or cream.

Fruit

If time is short or you are at a loss as to what to serve for dessert, simply serve fresh fruit. Whatever the season of the year there is always fresh fruit available, although there is a better selection in the summer. Choose fruit which is slightly under-ripe unless it is to be eaten immediately. If you are serving a bowl of fruit, include at least four varieties: apples, apricots, bananas, cherries, grapes, oranges, peaches or plums. Soft fruit is best served on its own with cream and sprinkled with caster sugar. Blackberries, currants, peaches, raspberries or strawberries are good; or try a combination of fruit; raspberries mixed with red currants are lovely. Other fruits which can be served on their own or as part of a fruit salad are grapefruit and orange segments, melon, passionfruit and pineapple. Some fruit must be cooked before serving, such as rhubarb, green gooseberries, and damsons, but the cooked fruit can be served hot or cold.

Stewed Fruit
Serves 3–4

Never cook fruit so that it becomes a pulp; each piece should still be recognisable. Choose any fruit which is in season. Peel, core and slice apples and pears; stone plums, apricots, damsons and other stoned fruit; wipe and slice rhubarb; top-and-tail gooseberries. Serve with custard or cream.

1 lb/½ kg prepared fruit
4 oz/100 g sugar or to taste
½ pint/3 dl water
thin strip of lemon rind or 2 cloves

Prepare the fruit. Put the sugar and water in a saucepan, heat gently, stirring until the sugar is dissolved. Add the lemon rind or cloves, then the fruit. Cover the pan and simmer until the fruit is tender.

Golden Fruit Salad
Serves 3–4

Use any fresh fruit in season. Oranges, bananas and apples make a good base and you can add others as available.

1 lb/½ kg fresh fruit
¼ pint/1½ dl golden syrup
orange juice

Prepare the fruit according to the variety. Put the syrup into a bowl and thin it with orange juice to taste. Pour the syrup over the fruit and toss lightly. Chill before serving.

Summer Pudding
Serves 6

A very fruity pudding which everyone likes and a good way of using up stale bread. Start preparing it the day before it is needed.

6 large slices stale bread
1½ lb/¾ kg soft fruit, berries, currants, rhubarb or cherries
4 oz/100 g sugar
4 tablespoons water

Cut the crusts off the bread and slice into fingers. Line the base and sides of a 2 pint/1¼ litre pudding basin. Prepare the fruit according to the variety. Put the sugar and water into a saucepan and heat, stirring until the sugar is dissolved. Add the fruit, cover the pan and cook until just tender (5–15 minutes according to the fruit; raspberries take the least time, blackcurrants and gooseberries the longest). Put half the hot fruit into the lined pudding basin, cover with more bread, then put in the remaining hot fruit. Cover the top with the rest of the bread. Put a saucer or small plate on top with a heavy weight to press it down. Cool, then put into the refrigerator overnight. Unmould onto a plate for serving with cream or custard.

Fruit Fool
Serves 4

For a more economical dish, use ½ pint/3 dl thick custard instead of the whipped cream.

1 quantity stewed fruit (use only 4 tablespoons water)
½ pint/3 dl whipping cream
food colouring (optional)

Prepare the stewed fruit as given on this page, using only 4 tablespoons water. Cool, then press through a sieve with a wooden spoon or blend until smooth in an electric blender. Whip the cream until stiff then, when the fruit purée is quite cold, fold the purée and cream gently but thoroughly together. Add a few drops of food colouring if the colour is pale. Chill before serving.

Dried Fruit

Dried fruits such as apple rings, pears, apricots, prunes, are a good store cupboard standby. They can be used instead of fresh fruit for nearly every recipe. They do need some special preparation.

Wash the fruit in warm water, then put into a bowl with warm water to cover. Leave to soak for 12–24 hours. Put the fruit and water in a saucepan and bring to the boil. Cover and simmer gently until tender. Stir in sugar to taste.

Pastry

The art of pastry making goes back for hundreds of years and had been perfected by the time of Queen Elizabeth 1. Today's cook has many aids unknown to our ancestors, but the basic principles remain the same and once having mastered these, she has the key to an endless variety of sweet and savoury dishes. Nor is it as difficult to make good pastry as some people seem to think, and the beginner who follows our simple instructions should be successful from the start. In the following pages we deal with shortcrust, rough puff and flaky pastry (few people nowadays think it worthwhile to make their own puff paste), suet crust, flan pastry, hot water crust and choux pastry. We start with shortcrust, the simplest and most often used.

Shortcrust Pastry

Plain shortcrust can be used in savoury or sweet dishes.

    8 oz/200 g plain flour
    pinch of salt
    2 oz/50 g margarine
    2 oz/50 g lard
    about 2 tablespoons water

1 Sift flour and salt together into a bowl. Use plain flour for a light, crisp crust. Self-raising flour makes a very cakey texture.

2 Add the fat, cut into pieces. Always use half as much fat as flour, preferably half lard and half margarine or butter. For economy use well clarified bacon fat or dripping.

3 Rub fat into flour with *cool* fingertips until the mixture resembles fine breadcrumbs. Stop rubbing in if the fat gets warm and starts to melt.

4 Add water carefully — about 1 teaspoon to 1 oz/ 25 g flour. Sprinkle it over the rubbed-in mixture and stir in with a round-bladed knife until the mixture is almost bound together, then gather it into a dough with your hand.

5 Put the dough on a floured surface and knead lightly.

Don't use too much flour when rolling it out. Roll gently, in one direction only, and turn the dough round occasionally. Shape the pastry, then leave in a cool place for about 30 minutes, especially on a hot day. Keep pastry as cool as possible at every stage. Bake as directed in the recipe.

Fruity Apple Dumplings
Serves 4
These are made with rich short-crust pastry.
Pastry:
8 oz/200 g plain flour
pinch of salt
2 oz/50 g margarine
2 oz/50 g lard
1 oz/25 g caster sugar
1 egg yolk
cold water to mix
extra caster sugar
Filling:
4 oz/100 g canned fruit (pine-apple, apricot, mandarin oranges are good)
1 oz/25 g raisins
1 level tablespoon soft brown sugar
4 cooking apples, peeled and cored
Make the pastry as for plain shortcrust up to the 'fine bread-crumbs' stage (no. 3). Stir in the sugar then the egg yolk, using a round-bladed knife. Add cold water to make a firm dough. Knead lightly and divide into 4. Roll each piece to a round about $\frac{1}{8}$ inch/$\frac{1}{4}$ cm thick. For the filling, drain the canned fruit. Chop fruit and raisins coarsely and mix with sugar. Place an apple on each round of pastry and fill the core holes with fruit mixture. Damp edges of pastry with water. Bring pastry up round apples without stretching it and press edges together firmly. Place the dumplings (with joins under-neath) on a greased baking tray. Brush with cold water and sprinkle extra caster sugar on top. Bake in a moderately hot oven (375°F/190°C/Mark 5) for 20 minutes, then reduce to 325°F/170°C/Mark 3 for 25 minutes or until apples are tender.

Cheese Straws
Use stale, dry cheese if possible for cheese pastry. It could also be used for covering a savoury pie, savoury flan cases or small cocktail savouries.
8 oz/200 g plain flour
pinch of salt
$\frac{1}{2}$ level teaspoon dry mustard
2 oz/50 g margarine
2 oz/50 g lard
4 oz/100 g cheese, grated
1 egg yolk
cold water to mix
Sift flour, salt and mustard, add fats and rub in as for plain short-crust. Stir in the cheese and egg yolk with a round-bladed knife. Add water to make a firm dough. Knead lightly on a floured board. Roll it out to $\frac{1}{4}$ inch/$\frac{1}{2}$ cm thick-ness. Cut into 3 inch/7 cm strips, then slice these into $\frac{1}{4}$ inch/$\frac{1}{2}$ cm straws. Shape some straws into rings. Place on a greased baking tray and bake in a hot oven (400°F/200°C/Mark 6) for 10–15 minutes or until golden. Serve bundles of straws pushed through rings.

Flaky Pastry

Flaky pastry can be used for both sweet and savoury dishes. It can make a light flaky topping for pies, or smaller items such as sausage rolls, Banbury cakes and apple turnovers. Keep all the utensils and ingredients as cold as possible and treat the pastry with a light touch. Flaky pastry needs care and time, but the finished product is well worth while

8 oz/200 g plain flour
pinch of salt
3 oz/75 g butter
3 oz/75 g lard
½ teaspoon lemon juice
about ¼ pint/1½ dl cold water

1 Sift the flour and salt into a bowl. Mash the butter and lard together until very well mixed, then shape into a block again. Cut the block into four. Add one of the pieces of fat to the flour and rub it into the flour with your fingertips. Sprinkle in the lemon juice, then add enough cold water to make a firm dough. Mix with a round-bladed knife until nearly all the dough is bound together, then use your fingers to gather all the pastry into one piece.

2 Knead the dough on a lightly floured surface until it is smooth. Put into a polythene bag and leave in a cold place, preferably the refrigerator, for about 30 minutes. Roll out the dough, again on a lightly floured surface, to a rectangle (about 12×6 inches/30×15 cm). Roll the dough evenly, pressing it at intervals with the rolling pin so as not to press out any air. Always roll away from you. Keep the sides straight and the corners square.

3 Mark the dough into three equal sections, without actually cutting the pastry. Take another portion of the fat and put small pieces of it over the top two-thirds of the pastry.

4 Fold the bottom third of pastry up over the middle, then the top third down. Press the edges together gently with the rolling pin, to seal. Give the dough a quarter turn to the left, repeat the rolling, add another portion of the fat as before and fold again. Cover the pastry with polythene and leave in a cool place for 30 minutes. Add the remaining portion of fat as before. Roll and fold once more without adding any fat. Cover with a piece of polythene and leave in a cool place for 30 minutes before using.

Rough Puff Pastry

This is very similar to flaky pastry but easier to make. The same ingredients are used but the fat is cut into $\frac{1}{4}$ inch/$\frac{1}{2}$ cm dice, and stirred into the flour. Add enough water to make a firm dough. Roll and fold as for flaky pastry, 4 times in all.

Bacon Sausage Rolls

Makes 15 large, 48 small sausage rolls. A delicious variation on the usual sausage roll recipe — the addition of herbs and bacon give the filling a distinctive flavour. Make small dainty sausage rolls (about 1 inch/2 cm long) for parties, larger ones (about 3 inches/$7\frac{1}{2}$ cm long) for family meals.

    12 oz/300 g sausagemeat
    6 rashers bacon, chopped
    1 level teaspoon mixed herbs
    salt and pepper
    8 oz/200 g flaky or rough puff
        pastry (made with 8 oz/200
        g flour etc)
    beaten egg for glazing

Put the sausagemeat, bacon, herbs, salt and pepper in a mixing bowl and mix together very thoroughly. Divide the sausagemeat into three and roll each portion into a roll 16 inches/40 cm long. Roll out the pastry on a lightly floured board to an oblong about 16 × 9 inches/40 × 23 cm. Cut the pastry into 3 strips, each 3 inches/$7\frac{1}{2}$ cm wide. Place a sausagemeat roll down the centre of each strip. Damp the long edge and either fold the pastry over or roll the sausagemeat in the pastry. Seal the pastry firmly. Brush with beaten egg. Snip at $\frac{1}{4}$–$\frac{1}{2}$ inch/$\frac{1}{2}$–1 cm intervals with a pair of scissors. Cut each roll into 16 small or 5 large sausage rolls. Put on a baking tray and bake in a hot oven (425°F/220°C/Mark 7) for 15–25 minutes (according to the size) or until cooked and golden.

Apple Sultana Turnovers

These light and crispy pasties can also be made as one large 'turnover' which is very impressive served with cream, for special occasions.

    1 lb/$\frac{1}{2}$ kg prepared cooking
        apples (peeled and cored)
    4 oz/100 g sultanas
    pinch of ground cinnamon
    2 oz/50 g soft brown sugar or
        to taste
    8 oz/200 g flaky or rough puff
        pastry
    caster sugar for sprinkling

Slice the apples and put them in a saucepan with 2 tablespoons water. Cover the pan and cook gently until soft and pulpy. Stir in the sultanas, cinnamon and sugar. Put aside to cool slightly. Roll out the pastry to an oblong about 10 × 15 inches/25 × 38 cm. Cut the pastry into six 5 inch/$12\frac{1}{2}$ cm squares. Divide the filling equally between the squares, damp the edges and fold the pastry over to make 6 triangles. Press together to seal and decorate the edges. Put on a baking tray, brush with water and sprinkle with caster sugar. Bake in a hot oven (425°F/220°C/Mark 7) for 30–35 minutes or until golden.

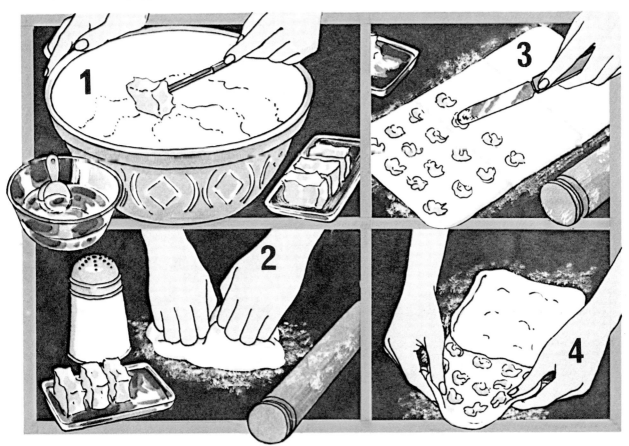

Suet Crust Pastry

If you are a real beginner, try suet crust pastry first. It is extremely good tempered and is very difficult to spoil. The only point that you must watch carefully is how you cook the pastry. If it is cooked too quickly, it will be hard and tough. For this reason, I would always steam suet crust pastry, never bake it. If you have a steamer this is ideal, otherwise the pudding or roll can actually be put into a large saucepan of boiling water. Make sure that the wrapping or covering is absolutely watertight or the pastry will become soggy. For hints on steaming see page 76.

You can use either ready-prepared shredded suet or fresh butcher's suet. Butcher's suet must be chopped before using and any skin and membranes removed. Sprinkle with a little of the weighed flour to make the suet easier to chop. Stir the suet into the flour, then add enough water to make a soft but not sticky dough.

Steak, Kidney and Mushroom Pudding

This is a very economical but tasty dinner. It is also very substantial — ideal for winter meals.
Pastry:
8 oz/200 g self-raising flour
1 level teaspoon salt
4 oz/100 g shredded suet
cold water to mix
Filling:
1 lb/½ kg chuck or blade steak
8 oz/200 g ox kidney
4 oz/100 g mushrooms
1 oz/25 g plain flour
salt and pepper
½ level teaspoon dried sage
3 tablespoons beef stock or water and beef stock cube

Make the pastry: Sift the flour and salt into a mixing bowl. Stir in the suet with a round-bladed knife then enough cold water to make a soft dough. Knead the pastry on a lightly floured board. Line a 2 pint/1 litre pudding basin with the pastry, leaving a piece for the lid.

Make the filling: Cut the steak into 1 inch/2 cm cubes. Wash the kidney very well and cut into pieces. Wash and slice the mushrooms. Season the flour with salt and pepper and sage and toss the meat and mushrooms in it until coated. Pack the filling into the pastry-lined pudding basin and add the stock. Cover the pudding with the pastry lid. Cover with a piece of greased greaseproof paper and a piece of foil, folded together with a pleat in the middle to allow the pudding to rise. Tie securely, making a handle of string over the top. Steam for 3—3½ hours.

Syrup Roly Poly

Serve with a lemon sauce or extra syrup. Children love it with a piece of butter melting on top.
Pastry:

    8 oz/200 g self-raising flour
    $\frac{1}{2}$ level teaspoon salt
    4 oz/100 g shredded suet
    cold water to mix

Filling:

    6 oz/150 g golden syrup
    1 oz/25 g fresh white bread-
      crumbs
    1 tablespoon lemon juice

Make the pastry: Sift the flour and salt into a mixing bowl, stir in the shredded suet with a round-bladed knife. Add enough water to make a soft dough. Knead the pastry on a lightly floured board then roll it out to a 10 × 10 inch/25 × 25 cm square. Make the filling: Mix the syrup, breadcrumbs and lemon juice together. Spread this mixture over the dough to within 1 inch/2 cm of the edges. Brush the edges with water and gently roll the pastry up like a Swiss roll. Press the edges of the pastry firmly to seal. Wrap the roll in greased greaseproof paper then in foil and seal well. Steam for 2 hours. Unwrap carefully and serve on a heated dish.

Lining a Pudding Basin with Pastry

1 Roll out the pastry to a round large enough to line the pudding basin plus $\frac{1}{2}$ inch/1 cm all round. Cut out $\frac{1}{4}$ section of the pastry and put it aside to form a lid later.

2 Damp the cut edges of the pastry then fit it into the pudding basin. Mould the pastry into the bowl until it is lined evenly. Press the

dampened edges together firmly. The pastry will stick up $\frac{1}{2}$ inch/1 cm all around the bowl.

3 Fill the lined bowl with a prepared sweet or savoury filling. Roll out the remaining $\frac{1}{4}$ pastry to a round to fit over the pudding.

4 Damp the edges of the pudding and place the lid in position. Press the edges together firmly.

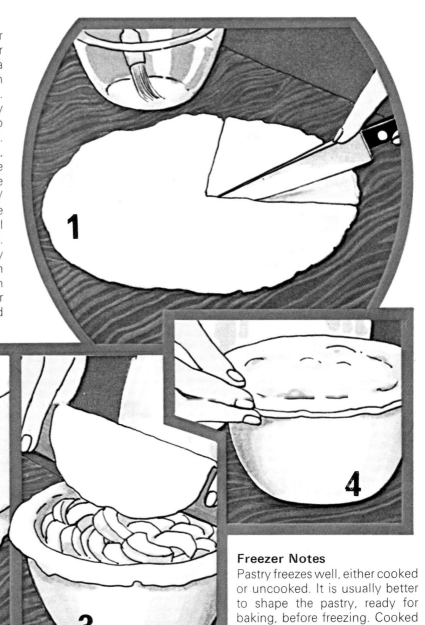

Freezer Notes

Pastry freezes well, either cooked or uncooked. It is usually better to shape the pastry, ready for baking, before freezing. Cooked pastry is very liable to become damaged so pack it in a rigid container.

Hot water Crust Pastry

Hot water crust pastry is traditionally used for making raised pies with a meat filling. Unlike most other pastries, this one should be kept warm all the time. Before you start, make sure that all the bowls and utensils are warm. Sift the flour and salt into the bowl and, if you have the time, leave this to warm as well.

Veal, Ham and Egg Pie
Serves 4–6
Always serve a raised pie cold. For a variation, use pork instead of the veal and bacon for a pork pie. A game pie can be made by using cooked and chopped game instead of the veal — keep the bacon for added flavour.

Filling:
12 oz/300 g stewing or pie veal (or 1 lb/½ kilo pork or cooked game)
4 oz/100 g bacon
rind and juice of 1 lemon
½ level teaspoon mixed dried herbs
salt and pepper
1 hard-boiled egg (omit if using game)
2 level teaspoons gelatine
¼ pint/1½ dl chicken stock, or water and chicken stock cube

Pastry:
10 oz/250 g plain flour
½ level teaspoon salt
4 oz/100 g lard
6 tablespoons water
beaten egg for glazing

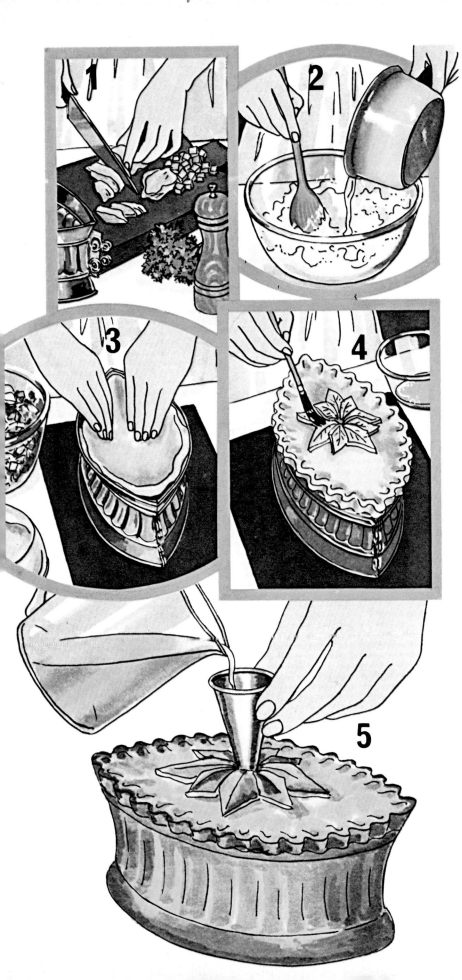

1 *Prepare the filling:* Chop the veal and bacon into small pieces. Mix with the rind and juice of the lemon, then herbs and salt and pepper.

2 *Make the pastry:* Sift the flour and salt into a mixing bowl and make a hollow in the centre. Heat the lard and water in a saucepan until the lard is melted, then bring to a fast boil. Pour the lard and water into the flour and stir well to make a soft dough.

3 *Shaping the pie:* Allow the pastry to cool slightly, then knead until smooth. Cut off about a quarter of the pastry for the lid and keep it warm until needed. Press the remaining pastry into an oval or round and lower it into a pie mould or 6 inch/15 cm deep cake tin. Mould the pastry until there is an even layer all over. There should be about $\frac{1}{2}$ inch/1 cm pastry above the edge of the mould.

4 *Filling and finishing the pie:* Put one-third of the prepared filling into the pastry-lined mould. Place the shelled hard-boiled egg on top and cover with the remaining filling. Press down well. Roll out the remaining pastry to form a lid. Brush the pastry edges of the pie with beaten egg, place the lid on top and press the edges firmly together. Trim the edges with scissors and crimp them neatly. Make any excess pastry into 'leaves', and arrange on the top of the pie. Make a hole in the centre. Brush the pie with beaten egg.

5 Bake in a moderately hot oven (375°F/190°C/Mark 5) for 1 hour. Remove the mould or cake tin, brush the sides of the pie with beaten egg and bake for a further 30 minutes. Allow the pie to cool. Meanwhile, dissolve the gelatine in the stock and pour into the pie through the hole in the top. The pie should be absolutely cold and the stock jellied, before it is served.

Choux Pastry

Choux pastry is very different from the other pastries. It is not rolled and shaped but spooned or piped into shapes. You do not need a light hand to make good choux pastry, but a strong arm to beat in the eggs. It is surprisingly easy to make, especially when you realise the dishes that it can produce — cream buns, éclairs, gougères, cheese aigrettes and so on. Plain flour is traditionally used for making choux pastry, but self-raising flour can be used if you wish to give the pastry a little extra lift and crispness. The air beaten into the eggs, plus steam from the water, causes the buns to rise to three or four times their original size when baked

Cream Buns and Eclairs

Makes about 10
Make sure that these are thoroughly cooked or they will collapse and be soft, not crisp and light. As soon as they are cooked, make a small slit in the side to let out the steam.
Pastry:
    $2\frac{1}{2}$ oz/65 g self-raising flour
    $\frac{1}{4}$ pint/$1\frac{1}{2}$ dl water
    2 oz/50 g butter or margarine
    2 eggs beaten
Filling and topping:
    $\frac{1}{4}$ pint/$1\frac{1}{2}$ dl whipped cream
    6 oz/175 g icing sugar
    1 level tablespoon cocoa
    hot water to mix
Make the pastry (see step-by-step instructions) and pipe it into 2–3 inch/5–7 cm lengths and $1\frac{1}{2}$ inch/4 cm diameter rounds on a baking tray. Bake in a hot oven (400°F/200°C/Mark 6) for about 35 minutes or until well-risen, golden and dry. Cool on a wire rack. Fill each bun or éclair with whipped cream. Sift the icing sugar and cocoa together, then beat in enough hot water to make a stiff coating icing. Cool. Dip the top of each bun or éclair into the icing, then leave to set.

Making Choux Pastry

1 Sift the flour. Put the water and butter in a saucepan, heat until the butter is melted, then bring the liquid to the boil. Add the flour all at once, then beat the mixture while it is gently cooking. Continue until the mixture forms a ball and leaves the pan clean.

2 Remove the saucepan from the heat then gradually beat in the eggs. Beat the mixture very well until thoroughly blended.

3 Spoon the pastry into a piping bag with a plain $\frac{1}{2}$ inch/1 cm pipe. Pipe the mixture, as shown, onto damp baking trays. Space the buns or éclairs to allow for rising. Bake as directed.

Cheese Aigrettes

These small, crisp, savoury balls are very good to serve at the end of a dinner party. They also make a good hot savoury for a buffet or cocktail party.
    $2\frac{1}{2}$ oz/65 g self-raising flour
    $\frac{1}{4}$ pint/$1\frac{1}{2}$ dl water
    2 oz/50 g butter or margarine
    2 eggs
    2 oz/50 g Parmesan cheese, grated
    $\frac{1}{2}$ level teaspoon made mustard
    oil for deep frying
    salt

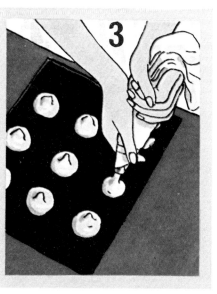

Make the choux pastry (see pictures) then beat in the Parmesan cheese and mustard until melted. Fill a deep frying pan one-third to half full of oil and heat it to 375°F/190°C/Mark 5 (a ½ inch/1 cm cube of bread will brown in ½ minute). Carefully drop teaspoonsful of the cheese choux pastry into the hot oil and fry for 5–10 minutes or until puffed up and well browned. Drain well on absorbent kitchen paper. Sprinkle with salt and serve piping hot. This mixture can also be baked to make éclairs and served with a savoury filling – pâté is good.

Sweet and Savoury Pies

Both sweet and savoury pies can have either a top and bottom crust or a top crust only. Use flaky or shortcrust pastry or bought puff pastry. It is important to choose a dish which is the right size, not only for the filling but also for the amount of pastry you are making. If the dish is too large or there is not enough filling, the pastry will be very thin and the top crust will sink. Too small a dish and the pastry will be much too thick. It is better to overfill a pie, especially with fruit, as it shrinks in cooking. When layering fruit and sugar, finish with a fruit layer because the sugar may make the pastry rather wet. For meat pies the filling is usually cooked first as the meat takes longer to become tender than the pastry takes to cook.

Top and bottom crust: Use a metal dish or plate if possible, otherwise the pastry may not cook properly underneath. If a rich shortcrust pastry or cheese pastry is being used, grease the pie plate. Roll out half of the prepared pastry to a round slightly larger than the plate and about $\frac{1}{8}$ inch/$\frac{1}{4}$ cm thick. Fold the pastry over the rolling pin onto the plate. Make sure that there is no air trapped underneath. Spread the filling over the pastry. Roll out the remaining pastry to a round slightly larger than plate. Damp the edges of the pastry, cover with the lid and press the edges very firmly together. Make a small cut in the top to allow steam to escape. Trim the edges and decorate as desired.

Top crust pie: Put plenty of filling in the pie dish. Roll out the pastry to the shape and size of the pie dish plus about $\frac{3}{4}$ inch/2 cm all round. Put the pie dish on the centre of the pastry and run a sharp knife at an angle around the edge. This will cut a strip from the pastry about $\frac{1}{2}$ inch/1 cm wide. Grease the edge of the dish and place the pastry strip on it. Press firmly, then damp it with water. Lift the pastry top, round the rolling pin, onto the pie. Press the edges onto the pastry strip. Trim.

Finishing the pie: Hold the pie in one hand and cut away the excess pastry with a sharp knife. Place the back of your forefinger just inside the cut edge of the pastry. Press down gently and make small horizontal cuts into the pastry edge with the knife, to give a flaky appearance. Flute the edges by placing your thumb on the flaked pastry edge, and at the same time make a shallow cut upwards beside your thumb. Do this at intervals all round the pie. Pastry trimmings can be made into leaf shapes to decorate the pie. Brush with beaten egg, milk or water to glaze. Sweet pies can be brushed with milk or water and sprinkled with sugar. Bake as directed in the particular recipe.

Apricot Pie · Serves 6

Any other fresh fruit in season or any canned fruit can be used for this pie with top and bottom crust.

8 oz/200 g shortcrust pastry (made with 8 oz/200 g flour etc.)
$1\frac{1}{2}$ lb/675 g apricots or 2 ($15\frac{1}{2}$ oz/439 g) cans apricots)
3 tablespoons apricot jam or 1 level tablespoon cornflour
milk for glazing

1 Heat the oven to 400°F/200°C/Mark 6. Roll out just over half of the pastry on a lightly floured surface and line a 7 inch/18 cm deep pie plate. Trim the edges.

2 Make the filling. Cook the apricots in boiling water for 2 minutes, then slip off the skins. Mix the fruit with the

3

jam. (If you use canned apricots drain them well and reserve ¼ pint/1½ dl syrup. Mix 2 tablespoons syrup with the cornflour in a saucepan, then blend in the rest of the syrup. Bring to the boil, stirring all the time until boiling and thickened. Cool, then mix with the drained apricots.) Put the filling in the pastry case.

3 Roll out the reserved pastry to the size of the

pie. Damp the edges of the pie and cover with the lid. Press the edges firmly together to seal. Flute them as described on opposite page. Cut a hole in the centre to allow steam to escape. Decorate with pastry leaves if liked. Brush with milk and bake in the preheated oven for about 40 minutes or until golden. Sprinkle with caster sugar and serve with cream or custard.

Lamb and Vegetable Pie
Serves 6

A very tasty pie with a flaky crust. As with most meat pies, the filling is cooked before being covered with the pastry. Shoulder of lamb is best for this recipe. A steak and kidney pie can be made by substituting 1½ lb/675 g chuck or blade steak and 8 oz/225 g ox kidney, cut into pieces, for the lamb, carrots and celery. If you want to use frozen puff pastry buy a 13 oz/369 g packet. For a pastry mix weigh out 14 oz/400 g.

   1 oz/25 g dripping or oil
   1 onion, chopped
   8 oz/225 g carrots, sliced
   2 sticks celery, sliced
   1½ lb/675 g boneless lamb, cut into 1 inch/2 cm cubes
   1 oz/25 g plain flour
   ½ pint/3 dl beef stock or water and beef stock cube
   salt and pepper
   1 bay leaf
   pinch of mixed dried herbs
   4 oz/100 g button mushrooms
   8 oz/200 g flaky pastry (made with 8 oz/200 g flour etc.)
   beaten egg

Heat the dripping in a large saucepan and fry the onion, carrots and celery until softened but not browned. Toss the lamb in the flour and add to the saucepan. Fry gently, stirring, until browned all over. Stir in the stock, scraping the bottom of the saucepan to remove any cooked flour. Add salt and pepper, bay leaf and herbs. Bring to the boil, then simmer for about 1 hour or until the meat is almost tender. Add the mushrooms. Spoon meat, mushrooms and liquid into a 1½ pint/9 dl pie dish and remove the bay leaf. Roll out the pastry on a lightly floured surface. Put the top crust on the pie (see opposite) and decorate with pastry 'leaves'. Make a hole in the top. Brush well with beaten egg and bake in a hot oven (425°F/220°C/Mark 7) for 25 minutes, then reduce the oven temperature to moderate (350°F/180°C/Mark 4) and bake for a further 15 minutes.

Flans

Flans are open top pies. The pastry is shaped into a flan ring which is standing on a baking tray. The flan ring is removed during the cooking so that the flan case is completely self-contained. Traditionally, a fluted flan ring is used for sweet flans, a plain one for those with savoury fillings. If you do not happen to have a flan ring, use a tart plate or cake tin, preferably a metal one. Use shortcrust pastry for flans: rich shortcrust for sweet; cheese pastry for savoury; plain shortcrust if time is short.

Baking a Flan Case

A flan can be baked with the filling already in it. Alternatively, bake the flan case 'blind' or empty, ready for a cold filling. The baking beans can be used over and over again, so don't throw them away.

Fruit Flans

Any fruit, fresh, cooked, frozen or canned can be placed in a rich shortcrust pastry flan case (baked 'blind'). Glaze the fruit with a little jam (apricot jam or red currant jelly is good). If the fruit is very juicy, brush a little jam on the base of the flan to stop the pastry from becoming soggy. Serve with cream.

1 Roll out the pastry on a lightly floured board to the size of the flan ring plus $1\frac{1}{2}$ inches/4 cm. Place the flan ring on a baking tray. Pick up the pastry over the rolling pin and gently place the pastry in the ring.

2 Ease the pastry into the corner of the ring and shape carefully without stretching. Roll your rolling pin across the top of the ring to cut off the excess pastry. To bake 'blind', prick the base then line the flan with greaseproof paper or foil and fill it with baking beans (usually haricot beans). Bake for 15 minutes, then carefully remove the beans, paper and ring. Cook for a further 10–15 minutes.

Hawaiian Pineapple Pie
Serves 6

A delicious flan, using a ready-cooked flan case which has been baked 'blind'. Top it with cream instead of meringue if liked.

    6 oz/150 g rich shortcrust
        pastry (made with 6 oz/
        150 g flour etc.)
    2 level tablespoons cornflour
    $\frac{1}{2}$ pint/3 dl pineapple juice
    juice of 1 lemon
    2 eggs, separated
    $\frac{1}{2}$ pint/3 dl pineapple pieces
    2 oz/50 g soft brown sugar
    4 oz/100 g caster sugar
    extra pineapple pieces, glacé
        cherries and angelica for
        decoration

Heat the oven to 400°F/200°C/Mark 6. Line with pastry an 8 inch/20 cm fluted flan ring, lightly greased and standing on a greased baking tray. Bake the flan case blind. Make the filling. In a saucepan blend the cornflour with a little pineapple juice to make a smooth paste. Blend in the remaining juice and the lemon juice. Bring to the boil, stirring all the time until thickened. Remove the pan from the heat and quickly stir in the egg yolks. Add the pineapple pieces and brown sugar. Put the filling into the flan case. Whisk the egg whites until stiff and whisk in half the caster sugar until stiff again. Fold in the remaining castor sugar. Pipe the meringue in rosettes all over the top of the flan. Bake in a moderate oven (350°F/180°C/Mark 4) for 15–20 minutes or until lightly tinted. Decorate and serve hot. If it is to be served cold, cook the meringue more slowly (see page 21). Pipe the meringue in rosettes to resemble the skin of a pineapple for special occasions.
Swiss Tart: Peel, core and slice 1$\frac{1}{2}$ lb/675 g cooking apples. Cook with 2 tablespoons water and the finely grated rind of 1 lemon. When tender, beat until puréed. Fill a baked flan case, then cover with meringue as for the Hawaiian Pineapple Pie.

Spanish Flan   Serves 6
A creamy flan which could be served for a meal starter or as a light lunch or supper. Serve while still puffed-up.

    6 oz/150 g shortcrust pastry
        (made with 6 oz/150 g
        flour etc)
    3 oz/75 g streaky bacon,
        chopped
    3 oz/75 g Lancashire or
        Cheddar cheese, grated
    10 Spanish stuffed green
        olives, halved
    2 eggs, beaten
    $\frac{1}{4}$ pint/1$\frac{1}{2}$ dl thin cream
    salt and pepper

Heat the oven to 350°F/180°C/Mark 4. Make the pastry and line an 8 inch/20 cm flan ring standing on a baking tray. Make the filling. Fry the bacon until just browned and spread it over the base of the flan. Cover with the cheese, then the olives Lightly beat the eggs and cream together, season, then pour them into the flan. Bake for about 25–30 minutes or until the filling is set, well risen and golden.

Scones

SURE & SIMPLE COOKING

Scones are very easy to make and bake. They are ideal to serve for tea, either small dainty scones when entertaining or large, rugged, cheesey ones for the family. Eat them while still warm if possible. If they have been cooked beforehand, pop them back in the oven for about 10 minutes to warm them through. Handle the scone dough as little as possible. I find I always make my best scones when I am in a hurry.

Tea Scones Makes 10–12 scones

There are a number of additions to this basic recipe which you might like to try. The plain scones are good, however, served with butter, jam and whipped cream.

8 oz/225 g self-raising flour
½ level teaspoon salt
2 oz/50 g margarine
about ¼ pint/1½ dl milk

Scones need not be put on a greased baking tray unless they contain sugar or cheese. Heat the oven to 425°F/220°C/Mark 7. Sift the flour and salt into a mixing bowl. Add the margarine and rub it in with your fingertips until well mixed in. Using a round-bladed knife, mix in enough milk to make a soft dough. Knead the dough lightly on a floured surface, then roll out to ½ inch/1 cm thick. Cut out the scones, using a 2 inch/5 cm pastry cutter. Dip the cutter into flour before cutting each scone to prevent sticking. Place on baking trays and brush the tops with a little milk. Bake in the preheated oven for 15 minutes or until well-risen, golden and cooked. Tap the scones underneath, they should sound hollow when cooked.

Honey Walnut Scones: Stir 4 level tablespoons honey and 2 oz/50 g chopped walnuts into the rubbed-in mixture.

Fruit Scones: Stir 1 oz/25 g caster sugar and 2 oz/50 g dried fruit (sultanas, currants, raisins, dates, apricots, chopped if necessary, or a mixture) into the rubbed-in mixture.

Spicy Scones: Stir ½ level teaspoon finely grated orange rind, ½ level teaspoon cinnamon and 1 oz/25 g caster sugar into the rubbed-in mixture.

Cheese Scones: Sift 1 level teaspoon mustard with the flour. Stir 2 oz/50 g dry Cheddar cheese, grated, into the rubbed-in mixture.

Wholewheat Scones
Replace 4 oz/100 g of the flour by 4 oz/100 g wholewheat self-raising flour.

Treacle Scones

This recipe relies on the treacle and bicarbonate of soda working together to make the scone rise. Golden syrup could be used instead of treacle.

8 oz/225 g plain flour
pinch each mixed spice and nutmeg
½ level teaspoon bicarbonate of soda
2 oz/50 g margarine
1 oz/25 g caster sugar
2 tablespoons treacle
¼ pint/1½ dl milk

Grease a baking tray. Heat the oven to 425°F/220°C/Mark 7. Sift the flour, spices and bicarbonate of soda into a mixing bowl. Add the margarine and rub it in with your fingertips until well mixed in. Stir in the sugar, treacle and enough milk to make a soft dough. Knead lightly on a floured surface and shape into a round about 1–1½ inch/2½–4 cm thick. Place the round on the baking tray and mark the top into 4 with a sharp knife. Brush the top with milk and bake in the preheated oven for about 20 minutes or until cooked.

Scotch Pancakes

These are also called Dropped Scones. They are very quick to make and should be eaten as soon as possible. Place a clean tea towel on a tray and fold it in half. Keep the pancakes warm between the folds. Serve with butter and jam, syrup or honey.

8 oz/225 g self-raising flour
½ level teaspoon salt
1 oz/25 g caster sugar
1 egg
½ pint/3 dl milk
lard for cooking

Sift the flour and salt into a mixing bowl, then stir in the sugar. Make a hollow in the centre, add the egg and stir in with a wooden spoon. Gradually add the milk, beating well to make a smooth batter. Grease a large frying pan or griddle with lard and heat. Drop spoonsful of the batter in rounds on the hot frying pan and cook until the bubbles on top burst and the pancakes are golden underneath. Turn the pancakes over and cook the other side until browned. They will take 3–4 minutes to cook.

COOKING

Cakes

Everybody makes cakes at some time or another whether it is for the family or for a special tea party. If you are not used to baking, your first try will probably be for a birthday party. Cakes made by the rubbing-in method are the plainest and easiest. Creamed cakes are the best ones for parties, for they are rich and moist and store well. Gingerbreads and other cakes made by melting the fat and sugar are also easy to make and keep extremely well — in fact, they actually improve with keeping for a short time. The most tricky cakes are those which are made by whisking. These are normally cakes for entertaining as they are very light and airy. Do follow the recipe carefully and prepare the cake tin properly.

Lining a Cake Tin
For a shallow tin, simply grease it and line the base with a single round of greased greaseproof paper. For a deep-sided tin, after greasing, line it completely, sides and base, with a double thickness of greased greaseproof paper.

1 Fold a strip of greaseproof paper in half lengthways and make sure that it is long enough to go right round the tin. Use two strips if necessary. The double strip should be 1½ inches/4 cm wider than the height of the tin. Fold up ½ inch/1 cm of the paper along the fold edge. Snip into the ½ inch/1 cm fold at ½ inch/1 cm intervals. Cut 2 rounds or squares of greaseproof paper the size of the base of the tin.

2 Grease the inside of the tin, place a round or square of paper in the base. Grease the strip of paper and arrange it snugly around the sides of the tin with the snipped fold overlapping on the base. Grease the first round or square of paper and place the second one on top. Grease this also.

Victoria Sandwich

Whatever the occasion, a creamed cake is always right. This recipe is a classic and can be cooked in many different forms. Besides being baked in two 7 inch/18 cm shallow round cake tins, it can also be cooked in a 7 inch/18 cm shallow square tin, an 8 inch/20 cm shallow round tin and a 6 inch/15 cm deep sided round tin. The cooking time will be longer for these cakes. This mixture will also make 18 small cakes, baked for 15–20 minutes in a moderately hot oven (375°F/190°C/Mark 5).

- 4 oz/100 g butter or margarine
- 4 oz/100 g caster sugar
- 2 eggs
- 4 oz/100 g self-raising flour

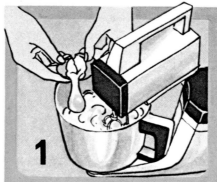

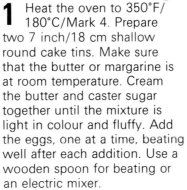

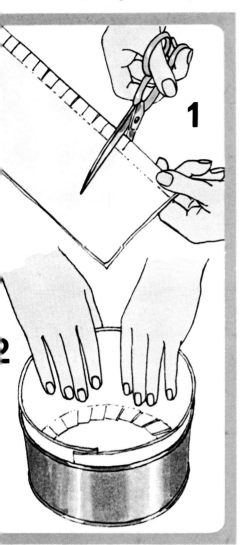

1 Heat the oven to 350°F/180°C/Mark 4. Prepare two 7 inch/18 cm shallow round cake tins. Make sure that the butter or margarine is at room temperature. Cream the butter and caster sugar together until the mixture is light in colour and fluffy. Add the eggs, one at a time, beating well after each addition. Use a wooden spoon for beating or an electric mixer.

2 Sift the flour, then fold it into the creamed mixture until thoroughly mixed in. You must not beat the mixture at all, and if you use a metal table spoon this will discourage any inclination to beat. Fold and cut the flour in carefully and very gently to avoid beating out any air which you have beaten in.

3 Divide the mixture between the two cake tins and bake in the preheated oven for 20–25 minutes or until well risen, golden and firm to touch. Allow the cakes to cool slightly, then turn them out onto a wire rack to cool.

When cold, fill the sandwich as liked — jam, jam and cream or butter icing (see page 108). Store any leftover icing in an airtight container.

Quick Mix Sponge Sandwich

Quick mix cakes are an absolute boon when time is short. I also find them almost foolproof. It is essential that you use the soft margarine that is sold in tubs. Fill as Victoria Sandwich.

- 4 oz/100 g self-raising flour
- 1 level teaspoon baking powder
- 4 oz/100 g caster sugar
- 4 oz/100 g soft margarine
- 2 eggs

Heat the oven to 325°F/170°C/Mark 3. Grease two 7 inch/18 cm round shallow cake tins and line the bases with greased greaseproof paper. Sift the flour and baking powder into a mixing bowl, add the sugar, margarine and eggs. Beat all the ingredients together with a wooden spoon for 2–3 minutes or until very well mixed. Divide the mixture between the two cake tins. Bake in the preheated oven for 25–35 minutes or until well risen, golden and firm to touch. Turn the cakes out of the tins and cool on a wire rack.

Flavourings for Victoria Sandwich or Quick Mix Sponge

Chocolate: Replace 2 level tablespoons of the weighed flour with cocoa.

Orange or lemon: Add the finely grated rind of $\frac{1}{2}$ orange or lemon with 2 teaspoons of the juice.

Vanilla, almond, peppermint: Add 1 teaspoon essence.

Rubbed-in Cake Mixtures & Gingerbread

If the children ask you if they may make a cake, get them to try one of these. Rubbed-in cakes are very simple to make, but unfortunately they do not keep well, and should be eaten as soon as possible.

Lemon Honey Tea Cake

Store any leftover in an airtight container. Next day serve sliced and buttered.

6 oz/175 g self-raising flour
4 oz/100 g margarine
4 oz/100 g granulated sugar
2 level tablespoons honey
finely grated rind of 1 lemon
2 eggs, beaten
3 tablespoons milk
Topping:
2 level tablespoons honey
juice of $\frac{1}{2}$ lemon

Heat the oven to 350°F/180°C/Mark 4. Grease a 1 lb/$\frac{1}{2}$ kg loaf tin. Line the base with greased greaseproof paper. Sift the flour into a mixing bowl. Add the margarine, cut into small pieces, and rub it into the flour with your fingertips until the mixture resembles fine breadcrumbs. Stir in the sugar, honey, lemon rind, eggs and milk. Spoon the mixture into the prepared tin and bake in the preheated oven for about 50 minutes or until well-risen and golden. Meanwhile, mix the topping ingredients together. Spread the topping over the cake as soon as it comes out of the oven, but leave the cake in the tin for about 10 minutes before transferring to a wire rack to cool.

Rock Cakes   Makes 16 cakes

These cakes are very plain. You can add 1 level teaspoon ground mixed spice, grated orange or lemon rind, or 4 oz/100 g dried fruit.

- 8 oz/225 g self-raising flour
- 1 level teaspoon baking powder
- 4 oz/100 g margarine
- 4 oz/100 g caster sugar
- 1 egg, beaten
- milk to mix

Heat the oven to 400°F/200°C/ Mark 6. Lightly grease a baking tray. Sift the flour, spice if used, and baking powder into a mixing bowl. Add the margarine, cut into pieces, and rub it into the flour with your fingertips until the mixture resembles fine bread-crumbs. Stir in the sugar, fruit if used, and egg, then enough milk to make a stiff mixture. Put 16 rough piles, well spaced, on the baking tray. Bake in the pre-heated oven for about 20 minutes or until well risen and golden. Remove from the baking tray and cool on a wire rack.

Gingerbread

Gingerbreads are as simple to make as rubbed-in mixtures. Don't keep them waiting, bake them as soon as they are made. They do however improve with keeping after they are cooked. Allow the gingerbread to cool completely, then put it in an air-tight container and keep for 2–3 days before eating; the flavour mellows. You can add 2–4 oz/ 50–100 g sultanas, currants, raisins or chopped dried apricots to the dry ingredients if you like a fruity gingerbread.

- 8 oz/225 g plain flour
- 2 level teaspoons ground ginger
- $\frac{1}{2}$ level teaspoon bicarbonate of soda
- $\frac{1}{2}$ level teaspoon salt
- 4 oz/100 g soft brown sugar
- 3 oz/75 g butter
- 6 oz/175 g treacle or syrup (or a mixture of the two)
- $\frac{1}{4}$ pint/1$\frac{1}{2}$ dl milk
- 1 egg.

Heat the oven to 325°F/170°C/ Mark 3. Line a 7 inch/18 cm deep square cake tin with greased greaseproof paper (see page 100). Sift the flour, ginger, bicarbonate of soda and salt into a mixing bowl. Put the sugar, butter and treacle or syrup into a saucepan and heat gently, stirring, until melted and thoroughly combined. Warm the milk and beat in the egg. Pour treacle mixture then milk and egg into flour and beat in with a wooden spoon. Pour into the prepared cake tin and bake in the pre-heated oven for 1–1$\frac{1}{2}$ hours or until well risen and firm to touch. Turn the cake out and cool on a wire rack.

Golden Syrup Buns

Makes about 24 small cakes

Small buns which are very good on their own but can be iced with orange glacé icing (see page 108) if liked.

- 4 oz/100 g butter
- 2 oz/50 g soft brown sugar
- 6 oz/175 g golden syrup
- 1 egg, beaten
- 8 oz/225 g self-raising flour
- 1 level teaspoon ground ginger

Heat the oven to 375°F/190°C/ Mark 5. Arrange 24 small paper cake cases on a baking tray. Put the butter, sugar and syrup into a saucepan and heat gently, stirring, until melted and combined. Allow to cool slightly, then beat in the egg. Sift the flour and ground ginger into the pan and stir until mixed in. Divide the mixture equally between the paper cases. Bake in the preheated oven for about 15 minutes or until well risen and firm to touch. Cool the cakes on a wire rack.

Fruit Cakes

A fruit cake which is rich and delicious and keeps well is popular with everyone — especially the cook. A very rich fruit cake is good for special occasions but probably too expensive for everyday family fare. These two recipes will stand you in good stead, whatever the occasion. Fruit is normally pre-washed when you buy it. If not, wash it in warm water and spread it on trays of absorbent kitchen paper to dry naturally. Do not try to hasten the drying or the fruit may become hard, but make sure that it is dry before you use it.

Plain Fruit Cake

You could use other dried fruit or nuts, dates, apricots, walnuts and so on as a variation to this basic recipe.

8 oz/225 g butter
1 level tablespoon black treacle
8 oz/225 g soft brown sugar
grated rind of ½ orange
4 eggs, beaten
6 oz/175 g self-raising flour
6 oz/175 g plain flour
4 oz/100 g raisins, chopped
4 oz/100 g sultanas
4 oz/100 g currants
2 oz/50 g glacé cherries, chopped
2 oz/50 g chopped mixed peel

Heat the oven to 325°F/170°C/Mark 3. Grease a 9 inch/23 cm deep round cake tin or 8 inch/20 cm deep square cake tin and line with greased greaseproof paper (see page 100). Have the butter at room temperature and put it into a mixing bowl with the treacle, sugar and orange

rind. Cream all together until lighter in colour and fluffy. Add the eggs gradually, beating well after each addition. Sift the flours and add them to the fruit and peel. Stir the flour and fruit into the creamed mixture. Spoon the cake mixture into the prepared tin and smooth the surface. Bake in the preheated oven for 45 minutes. Reduce the temperature to 300°F/150°C/Mark 2 and continue cooking for a further 1 hour or until well risen, golden and cooked (a skewer should come out clean). Turn out of the tin and cool on a wire rack.

Rich Fruit Cake

A dark rich cake for christenings, weddings, Christmas and other festive occasions. Use deep round tins, well lined with greased greaseproof paper. Use very dark brown sugar. If the cake mixture is not dark enough, add some gravy browning (Parisienne essence). Follow the table of ingredients according to the size of your tin.

Heat the oven to 325°F/170°C/Mark 3. Line the cake tin with greased greaseproof paper. Make sure that the butter is soft and at room temperature. Cream the butter and sugar together until lighter in colour and fluffy. Use your hand for large quantities of mixture. Add the beaten eggs gradually, beating well after each addition. Sift the flour with the spice and cocoa, mix with the grated lemon and orange rind and prepared fruit and nuts. Stir the flour mixture thoroughly into the creamed mixture. Add browning now, if needed. Put into the prepared tin and bake in the preheated oven for 30 minutes. Reduce the temperature to 300°F/150°C/Mark 2 for 1 hour. Reduce the oven temperature again to 275°F/140°C/Mark 1 until cooked. If the top of the cake overbrowns, place a piece of newspaper on top. To test if the cake is cooked, insert a skewer into the centre; it should come out clean and dry.

6 inch/15 cm	7 inch/18 cm	8 inch/20 cm	10 inch/25 cm	
4 oz/100 g	6 oz/175 g	8 oz/225 g	12 oz/350 g	butter
4 oz/100 g	6 oz/175 g	8 oz/225 g	12 oz/350 g	soft brown sugar
3	4	6	9	eggs
4 oz/100 g	6 oz/175 g	8 oz/225 g	12 oz/350 g	plain flour
1 level teaspoon	1½ level teaspoons	1½ level teaspoons	2 level teaspoons	mixed spice
½ level tablespoon	½ level tablespoon	1 level tablespoon	1 level tablespoon	cocoa
1	1	1½	2	oranges
1	1	1½	2	lemons
4 oz/100 g	6 oz/175 g	8 oz/225 g	12 oz/350 g	currants
4 oz/100 g	6 oz/175 g	8 oz/225 g	12 oz/350 g	sultanas
4 oz/100 g	6 oz/175 g	8 oz/225 g	12 oz/350 g	raisins, chopped
3 oz/75 g	4 oz/100 g	6 oz/175 g	8 oz/225 g	mixed peel
3 oz/75 g	4 oz/100 g	6 oz/175 g	8 oz/225 g	glacé cherries, chopped
2 oz/50 g	2 oz/50 g	3 oz/75 g	4 oz/100 g	almonds, chopped

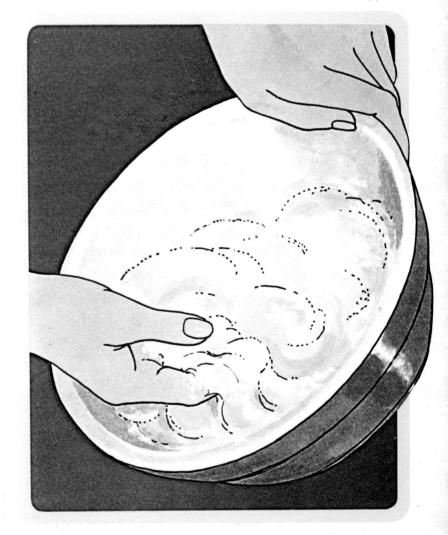

Whisked Cakes

Whisked cakes include those melt-in-the-mouth gateaux which can be served on high days and holidays. They should be light and airy but they do not keep very well, so they should be baked and served on the same day. They can be made with either plain or self-raising flour but I find that the latter gives them an extra lightness. The main factor in making these cakes rise, however, is the air that is whisked in with the sugar and eggs. Take care not to beat any of this air out when you fold in the flour; use a folding and cutting action with a metal tablespoon.

Swiss Roll

Whisked cakes are frequently baked as Swiss rolls which are slightly tricky to roll but as long as you bake the cake carefully and work very quickly once it has come out of the oven, you should have no difficulty.

Lining a Swiss Roll Tin

Place a double thickness of greaseproof paper on the work surface and put the tin on top. The paper should be about 2 inches/5 cm larger than the tin all round. With a pencil, mark the position of the corners of the tin on the paper.   Remove the tin and snip with a pair of scissors from the corners of the paper to the pencil marks.   Lightly grease both the tin and the paper and fit the paper into the tin. The pencil marks should fit into the corners and the paper overlap neatly to help the sides stand up.

Cake:
    3 eggs
    3 oz/75 g caster sugar
    3 oz/75 g self-raising flour
For rolling:
    extra caster sugar
Filling:
    3 tablespoons jam or butter icing (see page 108)

1 Heat the oven to 400°F/ 200°C/Mark 6. Grease and line a 9 × 12 inch/22 × 30 cm Swiss roll tin with greased greaseproof paper. Put the eggs and sugar into a heatproof mixing bowl.

2 Place the bowl over a saucepan of simmering water. The bowl should not actually touch the water. Whisk the eggs and sugar together until light, creamy and thickened enough for the whisk to leave a trail.

3 and **4** Sift the flour into the bowl and fold it in gently with a metal spoon.

Spread the cake mixture evenly into the prepared tin.

Bake in the preheated oven for 8–10 minutes or until well-risen and golden. Meanwhile wring a tea towel out in water and place it, doubled, on the work surface. Place a piece of greaseproof paper on top and sprinkle liberally with extra caster sugar. Put the jam for the filling into a saucepan and heat gently to soften.

5 As soon as the cake is cooked, turn it out of the tin onto the sugared grease-proof paper. Peel off the lining paper.

6 Quickly spread the cake with the jam, to come ½ inch/1 cm from the edge all round.

7 Using the sugared grease-proof paper, roll the cake up firmly. Place it on a wire rack, join underneath.

8 Allow to become completely cold, then trim the ends and serve sprinkled with more caster sugar.

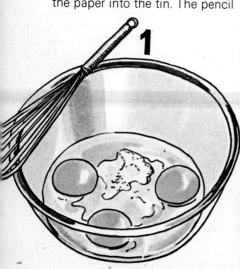

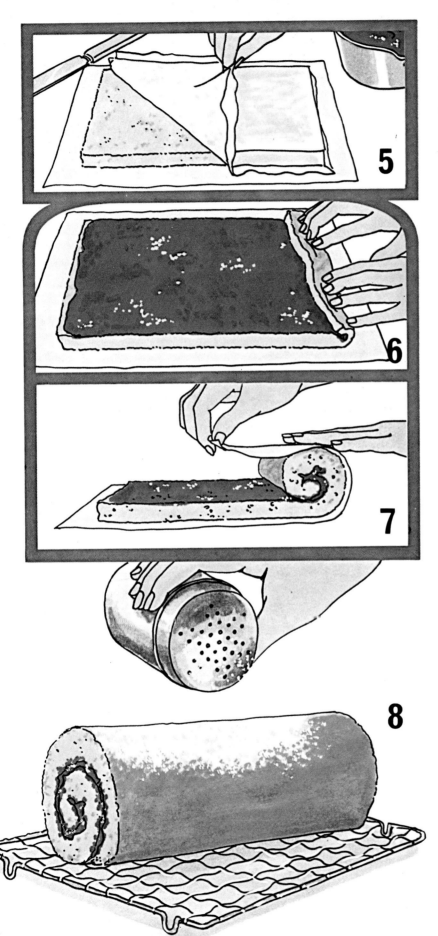

Butter Icing or Cream Filled Swiss Roll: Make in exactly the same way as for a jam Swiss roll but instead of the jam, roll the sugared paper into the cake roll. Allow the roll to cool, then gently unroll it, spread with icing or cream, and roll up again.

Strawberry Layer Cake

This sponge is good with any fruit, fresh or canned. The butter in the mixture makes a tighter texture but the cake will keep for a little longer. The whisked mixture must not get overheated. All the ingredients should be the same temperature when you fold in the flour etc.

Cake:

  3 eggs
  4 oz/100 g caster sugar
  4 oz/100 g self-raising flour
  1 oz/25 g butter, melted
  2 tablespoons warm water

Filling:

  $\frac{1}{4}$ pint/$1\frac{1}{2}$ dl whipped cream
  8 oz/225 g strawberries
  icing sugar

Heat the oven to 350°F/180°C/ Mark 4. Grease two 7 inch/18 cm shallow round cake tins and flour them lightly. Tap each tin upside down over the sink to get rid of excess flour. Put the eggs and caster sugar into a heatproof mixing bowl. Place the bowl over a saucepan of simmering water. Whisk the eggs and sugar together until light, creamy and thickened enough for the whisk to leave a trail. Sift the flour into the bowl and fold it in very gently and carefully, with the butter and water. Divide the cake mixture evenly between the two prepared cake tins and spread evenly. Bake in the preheated oven for about 20 minutes or until well risen, golden and firm to touch. Turn the cakes out of the tins and cool on a wire rack. Whip the cream, chop the strawberries. Fold the cream and strawberries together, adding icing sugar to taste. Sandwich the two cakes together with the strawberries and cream. Sift a little more icing sugar on top of the cake.

Cake Icings and Filling

The final touch to a beautifully made cake is the icing and filling. Most cakes can be served plain but on festive occasions, especially for children we like to add an icing.

Glacé Icing

A very basic and easy to make icing which can be used for almost any cake, rich, plain or fruit. It is also good for icing biscuits and buns.

8 oz/225g icing sugar
about 2 tablespoons boiling water
1 teaspoon lemon juice

Sift the icing sugar into a bowl. Add the boiling water and lemon juice and mix thoroughly. Use as soon as possible.

Orange or lemon glacé icing: Use all orange or lemon juice instead of water.

Chocolate or coffee glacé icing: Dissolve 1 level tablespoon cocoa or instant coffee in the boiling water. Omit the lemon juice.

Peppermint or almond glacé icing: Mix a few drops of essence into the finished icing.

Butter Icing

This recipe is enough to fill and ice the top of a 7 inch/18 cm sponge sandwich.

2 oz/50 g butter
4 oz/100 g icing sugar
2 teaspoons hot water
few drops vanilla essence

Put the butter in a mixing bowl and beat it until soft. Sift the icing sugar and gradually beat it into the butter. Beat in the hot water and vanilla essence.

Orange or lemon butter icing: Add the finely grated rind of $\frac{1}{2}$ orange or lemon. Use the juice instead of the water and vanilla essence.

Chocolate or coffee butter icing: Dissolve 1 level tablespoon cocoa or 2 level teaspoons instant coffee in the hot water.

Peppermint butter icing: Use peppermint essence instead of the vanilla essence. Add a few drops green colouring if liked.

Honeyed butter icing: Beat 1 tablespoon thick honey into the icing. This is especially good with orange or lemon butter icing.

Almond Paste

This is good to eat and less expensive than marzipan. Use it to cover a rich fruit cake (see page 105) before putting on the royal icing. This recipe is enough to cover an 8 inch/20 cm cake.

8 oz/225 g icing sugar, sifted
8 oz/225 g caster sugar
8 oz/225 g ground almonds
1 large egg
1 tablespoon lemon juice
$\frac{1}{2}$ teaspoon almond essence

Put all the ingredients into a mixing bowl and mix them together thoroughly to make a firm dough.

To Cover a Cake: Cut out 2 pieces of greaseproof paper, one the size of the top of the cake, the other long enough to go halfway round the cake, and twice the height of the cake in width. Roll out the almond paste to an even thickness, on the pieces of greaseproof. Brush the top and sides of the cake with apricot jam. Cut the long strip of almond paste in half to just the height of the cake. Put the two pieces around the cake. Cover the top of the cake with the other piece. Mould the almond paste around the cake, smoothing out the joins. Place the cake on a cake board and bring the almond paste down to touch the board all round. Leave to dry out for 1–2 days before putting on royal icing.

The illustrations show three ways of putting icing on a cake.

Top: Glacé icing is poured onto the top of the cake.

Centre: Spreading butter icing with a palette knife – this has a broad, thin, flexible blade.

Bottom: Piping rosettes of butter cream with an icing bag fitted with a large star pipe.

Royal Icing

A very white icing suitable for Christmas, birthday and other rich fruit cakes. This recipe is enough to cover an 8 inch/20 cm cake. The glycerine is available from chemist shops — do use it as it keeps the icing from becoming rock hard.

    3 large egg whites
    1½ lb/675 g icing sugar
    1 teaspoon glycerine
    juice of ½ lemon

Put the egg whites into a mixing bowl, sift the icing sugar into another. Add the icing sugar gradually to the egg whites, beating well with a wooden spoon after each addition. Add the glycerine and strained lemon juice. Continue beating until the icing is glossy and stands in soft peaks. Use as required. Keep the bowl covered with a damp tea towel while you are not using the icing, to prevent a skin forming. If the icing becomes too stiff, add a little more lemon juice. If you want it stiffer, perhaps for piping, add a little more sifted icing sugar.

Freezer Tip: The only cakes which are not worth freezing are gingerbreads and rich fruit cakes. Not that they can't be frozen — they can, but are just as easily stored in an airtight container. Freeze cakes as soon as they are cold. They can be filled and iced before freezing if liked. Plain cakes can be wrapped in foil, then put into a polythene bag. An iced cake should be frozen unwrapped until firm, then packed into a rigid container so that it doesn't get damaged in storage. I find that a Victoria sandwich mixture made in bulk (double or even four times the recipe) can be baked in many different ways and frozen. You then have a wide variety of cakes to choose from; small cakes, sandwich, ring cake, loaf, etc. Creamed cake mixtures can also be frozen unbaked, if necessary. Freeze in open cake tins lined with greased foil. When frozen, remove, wrap and seal.

Biscuits

Not many people make their own biscuits but they really are worthwhile — and very simple. Try any one of these recipes to prove it!

Basic Biscuit Mixture

Makes about 24 biscuits. These easy-to-make biscuits can be cut into lots of different shapes and the mixture can be flavoured as you like.

    4 oz/100 g butter
    4 oz/100 g caster sugar
    1 egg, beaten
    8 oz/225 g plain flour
    2 level teaspoons baking powder
    pinch of salt
    1 teaspoon vanilla essence

Put the butter and sugar into a mixing bowl and beat them together. Add the egg gradually, beating well after each addition. Sift the flour, baking powder and salt into the bowl. Add the vanilla essence. Stir all together to make a firm dough. Knead lightly, then wrap in polythene and put in the refrigerator for 1 hour. Heat the oven to 350°F/180°C/Mark 4. Grease two baking trays. Roll out biscuit dough thinly on a lightly floured surface. Cut out different shapes — rounds, squares, rectangles, triangles or use fancy cutters. Place on the baking trays and bake in the preheated oven for 10–15 minutes or until cooked. Transfer to a wire rack to cool.

The following varieties can all be made from the same basic mixture, adding special flavourings as given.

Chocolate Sandwich
Biscuits: Use 2 level tablespoons cocoa instead of that amount of flour. Sandwich two biscuits together with butter icing (see page 108).

Chocolate Peppermint
Biscuits: Use peppermint essence instead of vanilla. Dip the cold biscuits into melted chocolate to coat them.

Fruit Biscuits: Add the finely grated rind of ½ orange instead of the vanilla essence. Stir in 4 oz/100 g dried fruit (sultanas, currants, chopped raisins, chopped dried apricots, dates etc.).

Anzac Biscuits
Makes 30 biscuits
> 3 oz/75 g butter
> 3 oz/75 g granulated sugar
> 3 oz/75 g golden syrup
> 1 tablespoon hot water
> 1 level teaspoon bicarbonate of soda
> 4 oz/100 g plain flour
> 4 oz/100 g rolled oats
Heat the oven to 325°F/170°C/

Mark 3. Grease two baking trays. Put the butter and sugar in a mixing bowl and cream them together. Weigh out the golden syrup, then stir in the water. Gradually add all but 1 tablespoon of the syrup to the creamed mixture, beating all the time. Mix the bicarbonate of soda with the remaining 1 tablespoon syrup and beat in. Stir in the flour and rolled oats. Roll pieces of the dough into 1 inch/2 cm diameter balls. Place on the baking trays and press to flatten slightly. Bake in the preheated oven for about 15 minutes or until firm and golden. Transfer the biscuits to a wire rack to cool.

Ginger Nuts Makes 24 biscuits
Leave out the ginger for Golden Biscuits.
> 6 oz/175 g self-raising flour
> 1 level teaspoon bicarbonate of soda
> 1½ level teaspoons ground ginger
> 3 oz/75 g butter
> 2 oz/50 g granulated sugar
> 4 oz/100 g golden syrup
Heat the oven to 325°F/170°C/Mark 3. Grease two baking trays. Sift the flour, bicarbonate of soda and ginger into a mixing bowl. Add the butter and rub it in with your fingertips until the mixture resembles fine breadcrumbs. Stir in the sugar. Heat the golden syrup slightly, then pour it into the rubbed-in mixture and stir to make a firm dough. Divide the dough into 24

equal pieces and roll each into a small ball. Place the balls, well spaced, on the baking trays and press to flatten slightly. Bake in the preheated oven for 15 minutes or until golden and cooked. Transfer the biscuits to a wire rack to cool.

Chocolate Swirls
Makes 15 biscuits
For these pretty biscuits the mixture is piped onto the baking trays instead of being shaped with the hands or rolled out and cut. Use a large piping bag with a star piping nozzle.
> 6 oz/175 g butter
> 2 oz/50 g icing sugar
> 5 oz/150 g plain flour
> 1 oz/25 g cocoa
> few drops vanilla essence
> butter icing (see page 108)
> extra icing sugar
Heat the oven to 325°F/170°C/Mark 3. Grease two baking trays. Put the butter and sugar into a mixing bowl and beat them together. Sift the flour and cocoa into the bowl and stir in, with the vanilla essence. Put the mixture into the piping bag and pipe 30 small rosettes onto the baking trays. Bake in the preheated oven for about 15 minutes or until firm and cooked. Leave for 5 minutes before transferring to a wire rack to cool. When cold, sandwich the biscuits together with butter icing (try peppermint or orange flavour). Sprinkle with extra icing sugar before serving.

Cooking with Yeast

Cooking with yeast can take a little time but if you follow the recipes carefully it is very unlikely that you will have a failure. Yeast is a living organism and as long as it is not killed, it can withstand almost any ill treatment and still make a good dough for bread, buns and cakes. You can use either fresh or dried yeast, both will give equally good results. Fresh yeast can be kept in a loosely tied polythene bag in the refrigerator for up to 1 month. Dried yeast can be kept for several months but must be stored carefully. A cool dry place is ideal. As you use the yeast transfer it to a progressively smaller container so that there is the minimum of air space. When using the yeast it likes a warm atmosphere. Extremes of heat will kill yeast, cold will retard its growth. The flour you use will affect the texture of the bread. Use plain strong flour if possible although ordinary plain flour could be used in emergencies. Salt is an essential ingredient. It not only gives the dough flavour but also controls the yeast. Too much salt however will kill the yeast. Add sugar to the dry ingredients, except the small quantity needed for reconstituting dried yeast. Fresh yeast should not be creamed with sugar or the bread may have a yeasty taste. The fat in a recipe helps to keep it soft and stops it becoming stale so quickly.

Short-time White Bread

This method of bread making certainly saves time. You need to buy a bottle of ascorbic acid tablets. They are normally sold in hundreds (from most chemists) and are quite cheap.

- 1 oz/25 g fresh yeast or 1 level tablespoon dried yeast and 1 level teaspoon caster sugar.
- 14 fl oz/4 dl warm water
- 1 (25 mg) ascorbic acid tablet
- 1½ lb/675 g plain strong flour
- 1 level tablespoon salt
- 2 level teaspoons caster sugar
- ½ oz/15 g lard

1 Blend the fresh yeast with the water *or* dissolve the 1 level teaspoon caster sugar in the water, sprinkle the dried yeast on the top and leave until frothy, about 10 minutes. Crush the ascorbic acid tablet and dissolve it in the yeast liquid.

2 Mix the flour, salt and caster sugar together, rub in the lard. Mix in the yeast liquid with a wooden spoon, to make a firm dough, adding a little more flour if necessary. The dough should leave the sides of the bowl clean. Put the dough on a lightly floured surface and knead it until smooth, firm and elastic. Shape into a ball and put it into a lightly oiled polythene bag to relax for 5 minutes.

3 Shape as required, either one 2 lb/1 kg loaf, two 1 lb/½ kg loaves or 18 rolls. Place the loaves in greased tins, rolls on baking trays. Put into a lightly oiled polythene bag. Leave until doubled in size and springs back when lightly pressed with a floured finger. Loaves will take 45–50 minutes, rolls 30–40 minutes, in a warm place. It will take longer in a cool place.

4 Bake in a hot oven 425°F/220°C/Mark 7: the 2 lb/1 kg loaves take about 45–50 minutes; rolls about 20 minutes. The bread should be shrunk away from the tin, be golden brown and sound hollow when tapped underneath.

Speedy Wheatmeal Bread

Many people prefer a brown bread which has a coarser texture and more flavour.

½ oz/15 g fresh yeast or 2 level teaspoons dried yeast
½ pint/3 dl warm water
2 level teaspoons caster sugar
8 oz/225 g plain strong flour
8 oz/225 g wholewheat flour
2 level teaspoons salt
½ oz/15 g lard

Blend the fresh yeast with the warm water *or* dissolve 1 level teaspoon of the caster sugar in the water, sprinkle the dried yeast on top and leave until frothy, about 10 minutes. Mix the flours, salt and remaining sugar in a bowl and rub in the lard. Add the yeast liquid and mix in to make a soft dough. Knead on a lightly floured surface until smooth, about 5 minutes. Shape the dough into a 1 lb/½ kg loaf plus 6 small rolls. Put into greased tins and place in a large lightly oiled polythene bag. Leave until doubled in size and springs back when pressed with a floured finger. This could take 30 minutes in a warm place, 1½ hours at room temperature or up to 24 hours in the refrigerator. Bake in a hot oven (450°F/230°C/Mark 8): 1 lb/½ kg loaf 30–40 minutes; rolls about 20 minutes. Test as for white bread.

Bread and Buns

Yeast need not be used only for making plain bread but also for excellent buns and tea breads. The addition of egg, extra fat and sugar produces a rich dough for delicious and moist sweet tea breads and buns, suitable for special tea parties.

Shaping Dough

The way the dough is shaped gives bread a special identity. Most doughs, plain and rich, can be baked in any of these shapes. Use a dough made with 8 oz/225 g flour, rise and bake as given in the recipe.

Plait: Divide the dough into 3 pieces. Roll each piece into a sausage 12 inches/30 cm long. Gather the 3 ends together and press firmly. Plait in the normal way. Brush with egg, leave to rise. Sprinkle with caraway, poppy or sesame seeds if liked.

Crown: Divide the dough into 6 equal pieces. Shape into smooth balls and arrange in a lightly greased 6 inch/15 cm shallow cake tin. Glaze and rise as for a plait.

Flowerpot loaves: Use a 4–5 inch/10–12 cm flowerpot. Before using, grease it very well and bake it in a hot oven (400°F/200°C/Mark 6) for 20 minutes. This helps prevent sticking.

Fancy rolls: Use 2 oz/50 g dough for each roll. Clover leaf — Form the dough into 3 balls and place side by side. Cottage — Divide the dough into roughly two-thirds and one-third. Place the smaller on top of the larger and press lightly, then push a skewer down through the middle. Rise and bake.

Fruit Tea Bread and Buns

Makes two 1 lb/$\frac{1}{2}$ kg loaves or 12 buns

This dough can also be shaped into buns; bake for about 20 minutes. Dip the brush in water before putting into the honey for glazing.

> $1\frac{1}{2}$ oz/40 g fresh yeast or $1\frac{1}{2}$ level tablespoons dried yeast
> $\frac{1}{4}$ pint/$1\frac{1}{2}$ dl warm water
> 2 oz/50 g caster sugar
> 1 lb/$\frac{1}{2}$ kg plain strong flour
> 2 level teaspoons salt
> 1 level teaspoon ground mixed spice
> 1 oz/25 g lard
> $\frac{1}{4}$ pint/$1\frac{1}{2}$ dl warm milk
> 12 oz/350 g mixed dried fruit
> honey for glazing

Blend the fresh yeast into the warm water *or* dissolve 1 level teaspoon of the sugar in the water, sprinkle the dried yeast on top and leave until frothy, about 10 minutes. Put the remaining sugar, flour, salt and

mixed spice into a bowl and rub in the lard with your fingertips. Add the yeast liquid and milk to make a soft dough. Put onto a lightly floured surface and knead until smooth and elastic, about 5 minutes. Put into a lightly oiled polythene bag, tie the end loosely and leave until the dough is doubled in size. Again knead the dough and knead in the dried fruit. Divide the dough in half, flatten each piece and roll up like a Swiss roll to fit two lightly greased 1 lb/½ kg loaf tins, (or shape as liked). Place in oiled polythene bags and leave until doubled in size again and the dough springs back when gently pressed with a floured finger. Bake in a moderately hot oven (375°F/190°C/Mark 5) for 30–40 minutes or until golden and cooked. Brush the top with honey while still hot, then cool on a wire rack.

Lardy Cake

This is a plain dough which makes a very good tea cake. It can be served buttered if liked.

½ oz/15 g fresh yeast or 2 level teaspoons dried yeast
½ pint/3 dl warm water
6 oz/175 g soft brown sugar
1 lb/½ kg plain strong flour
1 level teaspoon salt
4½ oz/115 g lard

Blend the fresh yeast with the warm water *or* dissolve 1 level teaspoon of sugar in the water, sprinkle the dried yeast on top and put aside until frothy, about 10 minutes. Put the flour and salt into a mixing bowl and rub in ½ oz/15 g lard with your fingertips. Add yeast liquid to make a firm dough. Put on a lightly floured surface and knead until smooth and elastic, about 10 minutes. Place the dough in a lightly oiled polythene bag, tie loosely and leave in a warm place until doubled in size. Knead the dough again, then roll it out to an oblong about 6 × 8 inches/15 × 20 cm. Mark the dough into thirds and put 1½ oz/40 g of the lard over the top two-thirds of the dough. Sprinkle with 2 oz/50 g of the sugar. Fold the bottom third up over the middle third, then the top third down. Turn the dough a quarter turn to the left. Roll, fold and turn the dough once more, adding another 1½ oz/40 g of the lard and 2 oz/50 g sugar. Roll out the dough to a 6 inch/15 cm square.

Put onto a greased baking tray, cover with oiled polythene and leave until doubled in size and the dough springs back when pressed with a floured finger. Score the top with a sharp knife. Bake in a hot oven (400°F/200°C/Mark 6) for 20 minutes. Melt the remaining lard and brush liberally over the cake. Sprinkle with the remaining sugar and bake for a further 15–20 minutes or until cooked. Transfer to a wire rack to cool. Serve sliced.

Freezer Notes: Fresh yeast can be bought in bulk, then wrapped in 1 oz/25 g portions in polythene for freezing. To use, grate it into the liquid while still frozen. The dough can also be frozen, unbaked. Place dough in a lightly oiled polythene bag to rise. Knead, then freeze immediately. After thawing, knead and shape the dough, then rise again and bake as usual. Baked bread also freezes well, although the crust tends to come away from the loaf if it is very crusty. When cooled after baking, wrap in polythene or foil and freeze quickly. Storage times: Yeast, up to 1 year. Risen dough, up to 4 months. White and brown bread, up to 6 months. Fruit breads and buns, up to 4 months.

Drinks

It is so convenient to buy ready prepared bottled drinks that most of us have forgotten just how good home-made ones can be. Often the flavours are completely different. Lemonade made from fresh lemons and sweetened as you like it, is much tastier than the commercial variety. The children will love your own home-made ginger beer and you will have no difficulty keeping up with the demand — it is so easy to make. Serve glühwein for winter parties as a change from the more usual punch. Milk shakes are a must — not only children but grownups too will ask for more.

Fresh Lemonade
Makes about 2½ pints/1½ litres

Unlike most commercial lemonade, this not only tastes like real lemons but is very economical to make. Do not keep for more than 1 week.

- 3 large lemons
- 4 oz/100 g sugar or to taste
- 2 pints/1¼ litres boiling water

Wash the lemons thoroughly in warm water, scrubbing if necessary. Using a potato peeler, peel the lemon rind very thinly, being careful not to take any pith as this can make the drink bitter. Put the rind and sugar into a bowl and pour on the boiling water. Cover the bowl and leave until cold. Squeeze the juice from the lemons and add it to the cold liquid. Strain the lemonade into a jug. Chill before drinking.

Strawberry Milk Shake
Makes about 1½ pints/9 dl

A special treat for a hot day — you will have no trouble with the children not wanting to drink their milk!

- 8 oz/225 g strawberries
- 1 oz/25 g icing sugar
- 1 pint/6 dl milk
- few drops red food colouring
- ice cream

Reserve some of the strawberries for decoration. If you have an electric blender, blend the remaining strawberries with the icing sugar, milk and colouring until smooth. Or, press the strawberries through a sieve with a wooden spoon to make a purée, then whisk in the icing sugar, milk and colouring. Chill well in the refrigerator. Pour into 4 glasses, put a spoonful of ice cream on top and decorate with strawberries.

Ginger Beer
Makes about 10 pints/6 litres

Once you have started the ginger beer plant you can keep on making ginger beer from it. When you divide the plant, give half to a friend.

The plant:
- ½ pint/3 dl warm water
- juice of 1 large lemon
- 10 sultanas
- 1 level tablespoon sugar
- 2 level teaspoons ground ginger

To feed (every day for 1 week):
- 1 level tablespoon sugar
- 2 level teaspoons ground ginger

To make the drink:
- 1 pint/6 dl boiling water
- 1 lb/450 g sugar
- 6 pints/3½ litres cold water
- juice of 2 lemons

To make the ginger beer plant, put all the ingredients in a screw-top jar. Cover tightly, then put in a warm place for about 3 days or until the plant is gently bubbling. Feed the plant, as given, every day for 1 week. After 1 week, make the ginger beer. Put the boiling water and sugar into a bowl and stir until the sugar is dissolved.

Add the cold water. Stir in the lemon juice. Strain the ginger beer plant through a double thickness of muslin, squeezing out all the liquid. Do not throw away the residue. Stir the liquid into the bowl. Pour the ginger beer into bottles. Seal and keep for 3 days in a cool place before drinking. The residue in the muslin is now divided in half. Give one half away and put the other in the screw-top jar to start the process all over again. Add ½ pint/3 dl cold water and feed. Continue feeding every day for a week as before.

Glühwein
Serves about 12 people

A hot wine punch which is traditionally served when skiers come in from the snowy slopes. It is an ideal warming drink for any winter party — especially when snow is on the ground.

- 2 large bottles red wine
- 1 lemon
- 1 orange
- 2 oz/50 g sugar
- 4 cloves
- ½ level teaspoon ground nutmeg
- 2 sticks cinnamon
- 1 pint/6 dl lemonade

Put the wine into a saucepan. Wash the lemon and orange well, then peel very thinly with a potato peeler. Squeeze the lemon and orange juice. Add the peel and juices to the wine with all the remaining ingredients. Bring to the boil, then pour into a heated serving bowl. Serve with a ladle, while still piping hot.

SURE & SIMPLE COOKING

Preserving

Preserving is the art of keeping fruit and vegetables from one season to the next. There are many ways of doing this and most people prefer to turn their produce into home-made jams, chutneys and pickles. This does of course give the fruit and vegetables a slightly different use. If you want to store fruit and vegetables whole, they must be bottled or frozen. Both these are very successful ways of preserving but frozen fruit and vegetables do have a fresher flavour and keep their shape better.

Jams and Marmalade
Only use good quality ripe fruit or the set may not be good. A large wide pan is almost essential for boiling the jam rapidly when necessary. The jam can spit so the pan must be big enough for the jam only to half fill it, even when you have added the sugar. Choose one which is made of aluminium, stainless steel or enamelled. It should have a heavy base to help stop the jam burning. Have ready some suitable jam jars, with covers and rubber bands. Wash the jars very well before you begin then stand them upside down in a warm oven so that they are hot and completely dry when you need them. Use Cellophane covers with waxed discs for covering the jam.
To test for setting: When the jam is nearly ready for potting you will have to test it to see if it will set well when cold. There are various methods but the easiest is the wrinkle test. Put a saucer in a cool place. When you think that setting point has been reached, remove the pan from the heat and put a teaspoonful of the jam onto the saucer. Allow to cool slightly then push it gently with your finger — there should be a skin forming on top which will wrinkle if the jam is ready.

Strawberry Jam
Yields about 5 lb/2 kg jam
This is perhaps the most tricky jam to make but also one of the most popular. The lemon rind helps the jam to set.
  $3\frac{1}{2}$ lb/$1\frac{1}{2}$ kg strawberries
  2 lemons
  3 lb/$1\frac{1}{4}$ kg white sugar
Rinse the strawberries, remove the stalks. Put them into a preserving pan. Squeeze the juice from the lemons then chop the skins roughly and tie them with the pips in a piece of muslin. Put the lemon juice and muslin bag with the fruit. Heat the pan very gently, stirring, until the juice begins to run. Simmer very slowly until the strawberries are tender. Remove the muslin bag and squeeze out any juice. Add the sugar and stir until dissolved. Boil rapidly until setting point is reached, about 15–20 minutes, Allow the jam to cool slightly, pour into hot jars and place a waxed disc (cut to fit) on top. Cover with a Cellophane cover when cold.

118

Raspberry Jam

Yields about 5 lb/2 kg jam

3 lb/1¼ kg raspberries
3 lb/1¼ kg white sugar

Make in the same way as strawberry jam, without the lemon.

Blackcurrant Jam

Makes about 5 lb/2 kg

Make sure that the fruit is very tender before you add the sugar or the skins will be tough.

2 lb/800 g blackcurrants
1½ pints/¾ litre water
3 lb/1¼ kg white sugar

Remove the blackcurrants from the stems and rinse in warm water. Put them into the pan with the water. Bring to the boil and simmer until the currants are tender, about 45 minutes. Add the sugar and stir until dissolved. Boil rapidly until setting point is reached. Pour into hot clean jars, place a waxed disc (cut to fit) on top and cover with a cellophane cover.

Plum Jam

Makes about 5 lb/2 kg

3 lb/1¼ kg plums
1 pint/½ litre water
3 lb/1¼ kg white sugar

Make in the same way as blackcurrant jam. Only cook the plums for about 30 minutes. Skim off the stones with a perforated spoon before potting.

Three Fruit Marmalade

Yields about 10 lb/4 kg marmalade

This marmalade can be made at any time of the year. The flavour is excellent. The total weight of the fruit should be 3 lb/1¼ kg.

2 oranges
4 lemons
2 grapefruit
6 pints/3 litres water
6 lb/2½ kg white sugar

Wash the fruit well in warm water. Cut in half and squeeze out the juices. If the pith is very thick, cut it away. Slice the skin into matchstick strips. Tie the pith and pips loosely in a piece of muslin. Place the juice, sliced fruit skins, muslin bag and water in the preserving pan. Bring to the boil then simmer until the skins are tender, about 2 hours. Remove the muslin bag and squeeze out the juice. Add the sugar and stir until dissolved. Boil rapidly until setting point is reached. Skim. Allow to cool slightly then pour into the prepared jars. Place a waxed disc on top of each jar. Cover, with Cellophane, when cold.

Seville Orange Marmalade

Yields about 10 lb/4 kg marmalade

Bitter oranges have the best flavour for an orange marmalade. The peel can be minced for speed.

3 lb/1¼ kg Seville oranges
6 pints/3 litres water
juice of 2 lemons
6 lb/2½ kg white sugar

Make as Three Fruit Marmalade.

Chutneys and Pickles

A pickle is a fruit or vegetable preserved in spiced vinegar. You must use perfect fruit and vegetables as they are still whole when the pickle is complete. Chutneys on the other hand can be made from misshapen and imperfect fruit and vegetables. The ingredients for chutney are chopped or minced very finely so that the finished chutney is a thick mass with no one ingredient recognisable. Use an enamelled or stainless steel pan. Aluminium pans must be scoured first very well if they are to be used for vinegar.

Spiced Vinegar

All chutneys and pickles are made with vinegar. Frequently the vinegar is spiced. Either make a good supply at the beginning of the preserving season or make it as you need it. Buy a ready mix of whole pickling spice or make your own mixture Try this one:

  2 inch/5 cm stick cinnamon
  10 cloves
  2 blades mace
  12 allspice
  12 peppercorns
  2 pints/1$\frac{1}{4}$ litre malt vinegar

Either put the spices in the bottle of vinegar and leave for 6–8 weeks then strain the vinegar. Alternatively, put the spices and vinegar into a heatproof bowl. Place the bowl over a saucepan of cold water, bring to the boil then remove the pan from the heat and allow the spices to steep in the warm vinegar for 2 hours. Strain the vinegar.

Green Tomato Chutney

Yields about 5$\frac{1}{2}$ lb/2$\frac{1}{2}$ kg chutney
An ideal way of using up any tomatoes that are not ripened at the end of the season.

1 lb/$\frac{1}{2}$ kg onions, peeled and chopped
3 lb/1$\frac{1}{4}$ kg green tomatoes, chopped
8 oz/225 g raisins, chopped
1 lb/$\frac{1}{2}$ kg cooking apples, peeled, cored and chopped
2 level tablespoons salt
12 oz/350g granulated sugar
1$\frac{1}{2}$ pints/9 dl spiced vinegar

Put the onions in a saucepan with water to cover. Bring to the boil then simmer until tender. Drain. Put all the ingredients in the preserving pan. Bring to the boil, stirring until the sugar is dissolved. Cook, uncovered, stirring occasionally, until thickened. Pour into hot clean jars and seal. Keep for at least 2 months.

Dried Apricot Chutney

Yields about 3$\frac{1}{2}$ lb/1$\frac{1}{2}$ kg
A deliciously different chutney that can be made at any time of the year.

  8 oz/225 g dried apricots
  8 oz/225 g tomatoes
  1 lb/$\frac{1}{2}$ kg onions
  8 oz/225 g granulated sugar
  grated rind and juice of 1 orange
  4 oz/100 g sultanas
  2 level teaspoons salt
  1 clove garlic, crushed
  1 level tablespoon dry mustard
  $\frac{3}{4}$ pint/9 dl spiced vinegar

Put the apricots in a bowl, cover with cold water and leave overnight. Next day, drain the apricots and chop finely. Put the tomatoes into a bowl, cover with boiling water and leave for 2 minutes. Drain, then rinse in cold water and peel off the skins. Chop the tomatoes finely. Chop the onions finely or grate coarsely. Put the onion in a saucepan with water to cover. Bring to the boil then simmer until tender. Drain well. Put all the ingredients in the preserving pan, bring to the boil, stirring all the time. Simmer the chutney, uncovered, stirring occasionally until thickened and there is very little excess liquid, about 2 hours. Pour into hot jars (see page 118) and seal. Keep for at least 1 month before using.

Pickled Onions

Use a stainless steel knife for peeling the onions or they may become discoloured.

    pickling onions
    cooking salt
    water
    spiced vinegar

Peel the onions. Make brine by stirring 8 oz/225 g salt into each 4 pints/$2\frac{1}{2}$ litres water, making sure that the salt dissolves. Cover the peeled onions with the brine. They will float so put a plate on top to hold them down. Put aside for 24–36 hours. Drain the onions well then pack them into clean jars. Add enough cold spiced vinegar to cover the onions by $\frac{1}{2}$–1 inch/1–3 cm. Seal. Keep the onions for at least 3 months before using.

Dill Pickled Cucumber

Use distilled white malt vinegar instead of brown malt vinegar when making the spiced vinegar for this recipe. Courgettes (zucchini) are also good pickled this way.

    cucumbers
    cooking salt
    water
    spiced vinegar
    dill seeds

Wash the cucumbers and slice into $\frac{1}{4}$–$\frac{1}{2}$ inch/$\frac{1}{2}$–1 cm slices, or cut into quarters then into shorter lengths. Make brine by stirring

3 oz/225 g salt into each 4 pints/$2\frac{1}{2}$ litres water. Cover the prepared cucumber with brine, keeping it submerged with a plate. Leave for 24 hours. Drain the cucumber and pack into jars. Cover with cold spiced vinegar. Put 1 level teaspoon dill seed into each 1 lb/$\frac{1}{2}$ kg jar. Seal. Keep for at least 1 week before using.

Bottling Fruit and Vegetables

Bottled fruits can be kept from one season to the next. They are an excellent standby for pie fillings or can be served on their own. They cost very little to process and, unlike frozen fruit, nothing to store.

Preparing Fruit and Syrup

Choose very fresh fruit which is perfect and just ripe. Prepare it as you would if you were going to stew it for eating straight away. The fruit is normally bottled in a syrup. Water can be used but the fruit tends to lose colour and flavour very quickly. For the syrup, as a general rule use 8 oz/225 g granulated or loaf sugar to each 1 pint/6 dl water. Bring to the boil, stirring all the time until the sugar is dissolved, then boil for 1 minute. If the fruit is very tart, you may need extra sugar but this can be added later when you use the fruit, if preferred.

Packing the Jars

You can use jars which are sealed either with a spring-clip or with a screw-band. Both rely on a rubber ring for a perfect seal. Use new ones every time as they do stretch with use. Soak them in warm water, then dip in boiling water just before using. Use scrupulously clean jars and test the seal before using. To do this, fill the jars with water, cover and seal. Hold the jars upside down over the draining board — any leaking should stop very quickly. Fill the jars with as much fruit as you can get in without bruising or spoiling it in any way. When packing soft fruit, place the jar on a tea towel and tap it gently every so often to dislodge any air bubbles which have become trapped.

Processing the Fruit

There are many different ways of processing bottled fruit. This method may not be the quickest but gives the best results. You need a large deep pan such as a pressure cooker or fish kettle. The pan must have a false base (a wad of newspapers will do) or the jars may crack on the hot metal. You also need a thermometer; buy one which can double up for testing hot oil for deep frying and for making con-

fectionery. Pack the jars and fill with cold syrup to cover the fruit. Put the sealing ring in position and cover but do not seal (tighten screw-bands, then release a quarter turn). Put the jars in the pan and cover with cold water. Heat very gently — the water should take $1\frac{1}{2}$ hours to reach the required temperature or the fruit may split. Carefully maintain this temperature as given below. Remove the jars from the water, and place them on newspaper to stop the jars from cracking. Tighten screwbands or put on the spring clips straight away.

Processing Times
Apple quarters, blackberries, currants, gooseberries, logan-berries, raspberries, rhubarb, strawberries: Heat to 165°F/74°C and maintain for 10 minutes.
Apricots, cherries, damsons, plums, peaches. Heat to 180°F/82°C and maintain for 15 minutes.
Pears, tomatoes: Heat to 190°F/88°C and maintain for 30–40 minutes (depending on how tightly they are packed).

Bottling Vegetables
Do not try to bottle vegetables unless you have a pressure cooker.

Vegetables for bottling must be just mature and as perfect in colour and shape as possible. For best results, grade them so that each jar is filled with vegetables that are almost identical. Prepare the vegetables as you would if you were going to cook and eat them straight away, but they must be scalded in boiling salted water before bottling. Times are given below. The vegetables are then packed into the jars and covered with boiling brine. The brine is made by dissolving $\frac{1}{2}$–1 oz/15–25 g cooking salt in each 2 pints/$1\frac{1}{4}$ litres water.

Processing Vegetables
The jars and seals used for bottling vegetables are the same as for fruit. They must however be robust enough to withstand 10 lb/$4\frac{1}{2}$ kg pressure in a pressure cooker. Fill the jars as tightly as possible without damaging the vegetables. Fill up completely with boiling brine. Cover but do not seal. Tighten screw-bands, then loosen a quarter turn. Put 2 inches/5 cm water in the pressure cooker, place the jars on the rack. Cover

and heat until steam comes out, continue for 7 minutes. Bring up to 10 lb/$4\frac{1}{2}$ kg pressure and maintain as required (see below). Allow to cool naturally, then seal the jars.

Scalding and Processing Times
(1 pint/6 dl capacity jars)
Asparagus: Scald 2–4 minutes according to thickness of stems. Process 30 minutes.
Broad beans, French beans, runner beans: Scald 2–3 minutes Process 35 minutes.
Young carrots: Scald 5–10 minutes according to size. Process 35 minutes.
Celery: Scald 3–5 minutes. Process 35 minutes.
Courgettes (zucchini): Scald 1 minute. Process 30 minutes.

Using Bottled Vegetables
Reheat vegetables in the bottling brine and serve as you would fresh vegetables. When you open the vegetables there should be no hiss of escaping gas. If there is, or the vegetables look or smell unsavoury, discard them without tasting.

Freezing Fruit and Vegetables

Without a doubt freezing is the best way for you to preserve fruit and vegetables. They can be stored in the home freezer for up to 12 months, i.e. you can keep your produce throughout the year until the next crop is ready.

When to freeze: During the spring and summer, make sure that you have space in the freezer to take all the fruit and vegetables that are at their peak and plentiful at that time. Most produce seems to be at its best simultaneously and only perfect fruit and vegetables are worth freezing. Pick and freeze on the same day — the less time lag the better. For this reason it is best if you grow it yourself, although many farmers now like you to pick your own from their fields.

Apples are sometimes tricky to freeze. Follow these simple instructions

Peel, core and slice the apples into salt water (1 level tablespoon to each 1 pint/6 dl) to help prevent browning. Do not leave for more than 10 minutes.

Blanch the apples (cook for 2–3 minutes) in steam preferably, to prevent further browning.

Using 4 oz/125 g caster sugar to each 1 lb/$\frac{1}{2}$ kg prepared apples, layer the prepared apple slices with sugar in rigid containers. You could also freeze the apples in syrup but mix in 200–300 mg ascorbic acid to the syrup of each 1 lb/$\frac{1}{2}$ kg pack. They can also be frozen as a purée; allow 3–4 oz/75–125 g sugar to 1 lb/$\frac{1}{2}$ kg prepared fruit.

Freezing Fruit

Switch on the 'fast-freeze' of your freezer some hours in advance if you are planning to freeze in a large amount. Prepare the fruit as you would for eating straight away. Decide which of these three methods you will use and freeze accordingly.

Unsweetened open freezing: Spread the fruit in a single layer on a tray, freeze until firm. Pack the fruit into airtight containers, label and store. Each piece of fruit is separate, so you can use as much or as little as you like at one time. The storage time is limited to 3–4 months however. Use this method for raspberries, strawberries, blackberries, cranberries and gooseberries.

Dry sugar packaging: Prepare the fruit, then using 1 lb/$\frac{1}{2}$ kg caster sugar to each 4 lb/2 kg fruit, gently mix the fruit with the sugar. Mix only in small amounts to prevent damage to the fruit. Leave for a few minutes. Pack into rigid containers, leaving $\frac{1}{2}$ inch/1 cm headspace for ex-pansion. Use this method for raspberries, strawberries, bilberries, blackberries, gooseberries, grapefruit segments, rhubarb.

Syrup packaging: Make a syrup the day before so that it can cool and then be chilled before using. Prepare the fruit and allow $\frac{1}{2}$ pint/3 dl syrup to each 1 lb/$\frac{1}{2}$ kg fruit. Mix the fruit and syrup, then pack in usable amounts in rigid containers. Place a piece of crumpled wax paper on the fruit to keep it submerged, then cover, seal and label. Use a heavy syrup (2$\frac{1}{4}$ lb/900 g sugar to 2 pints/1$\frac{1}{4}$ litre water) for blackberries, gooseberries, cranberries, plums and grapefruit segments; a medium syrup (1$\frac{1}{4}$ lb/500 g sugar to 2 pints/1$\frac{1}{4}$ litre water) for apples, apricots, bilberries, melon, peaches, pears, raspberries and strawberries; a light syrup (1 lb/400 g sugar to 2 pints/1$\frac{1}{4}$ litre water) for grapes, pineapple and cherries.

Freezing Vegetables

Switch on the fast freeze on your freezer if you are freezing in a lot of vegetables. Prepare the vegetables as you would if you were going to cook and eat them straight away. Put on a large saucepan of water to boil. Prepare a bowl of cold water with ice cubes in it. Place not more than 1 lb/$\frac{1}{2}$ kg vegetables in a blanching basket and immerse in the boiling water. Blanch for the following times (from the time the water returns to the boil) Peas: 1 minute. Runner beans (sliced) and diced carrots: 2 minutes. French beans, broad beans, broccoli flowerets, small brussels sprouts and whole small spring carrots: 3 minutes. After blanching, cool the vegetables in the iced water. Drain and dry as much as possible. Either pack the vegetables, in usable amounts, in rigid containers, polythene bags, or spread them out on trays to freeze before packing. Seal and label. Potatoes can also be frozen; blanch them in deep hot oil or fat, not water,

Index

A

Almond Paste	108
Anzac Biscuits	111
Apple Dumplings, Fruity	85
Sauce	63
Sultana Turnovers	87
Apples, Baked	80
Apricot Chutney, Dried	120–121
Orange Flummery	71
Pie	94–95
Trifle, Family	68

B

Bacon and Herb Stuffing	46
, Boiled	41
, Buying	33
, Roast	35
Sausage Rolls	87
Baked Apples	80
Egg Custard	18
Eggs	14
Fish	28
Fruit Pudding	80–81
Potatoes in their Jackets	51
Rice Pudding	74–75
Barbecue Marinade	47
Basic Biscuit Mixture	110–111
Batter puddings	17
Batters	16–17
Béarnaise Sauce	61
Béchamel Sauce	59
Beefburgers	42–43
Beef and Dumplings, Boiled	40
, Buying	33
, Casseroled	38
, Flemish Stew	38
, Frying and Grilling	36
, Roast	34
Stew, French	38
Beetroot Salad	53
Biscuits	110–111
Blackcurrant Jam	119
Blintz	17
Boiled Eggs	14
Bacon	41
Beef and Dumplings	40
Boiling Meat	40–41
Bolognese Sauce	55
Bottling Fruit and Vegetables	122–123
Brandy Butter	65
Bread and Buns	114–115
and Butter Pudding	75
Sauce	63
, Short-time White	112
, Speedy Wheatmeal	113
Brown Coating Sauce	59
Buns, Bread and	114–115
Butter Icing	108
Butterscotch Sundae	72

C

Cakes	100–109
, Creamed	100–101
, Freezer Tips	109
, Fruit	104–105
, Icings and Fillings	108–109
, Rubbed-in and Gingerbreads	102–103
, Whisked	106–107
Caramel Vienna Pudding	75
Casseroled Beef	38
Chicken	39
Lamb	38
Pork	39
Potatoes	51

Casseroles, Stews and	38–39
Cauliflower Cheese, Danish Blue	23
Cheese	22–23
Aigrettes	92–93
, Macaroni	55
Sauce	59
Scones	99
Slice	22·23
Soufflé, Hot	21
Straws	85
Cheesecake, Heavenly	69
Cheesy Cod Cutlets, Grilled	29
Chicken and Leek Broth	11
and Rice Salad Ring	56–57
, Casseroled	39
, Spanish	39
with Mushrooms	39
Chinese Pork	39
Chocolate Ice Cream	72
Chocolate Orange Mousse or Soufflé	67
Peppermint Biscuits	111
Sandwich Biscuits	111
Sauce	65
Semolina, Fluffy	75
Swirls	111
Choux Pastry	92–93
Christmas Pudding	76
Clams	27
Cockles	27
Coconut Syrup Pudding	78
Cod Cutlets, Cheesy Grilled	29
Cold Desserts	66–73
, Freezer Note	71
Coleslaw	53
Court Bouillon	29
Crab	27
Crawfish	26
Cream Buns	92
of Celery Soup	12
Crème Caramel	19
Cucumber, Dill Pickled	121
Curried, Lamb	38
Curry Rice	56

D

Dairy Desserts, Cold	68–69
Ice Cream	72
Danish Blue Cauliflower Cheese	23
Devilled Kidneys	44
Dill Pickled Cucumber	121
Dressing a Crab	27
Dried Apricot Chutney	120–121
Fruit	83
Drinks	116–117
Duchesse Potatoes	51
Dumplings, Boiled Beef and	40

E

Eclairs	92
Egg Based Sauces, Savoury	60–61
Jelly, Orange	70
Egg Custard	18–19
Sauce	18
Tart	19
Eggs	14–21
Eve's Pudding	81

F

Family Apricot Trifle	68
Fish	24–31
Cakes	30
Meunière	29
Niçoise	29
Pie	31
, Preparing	24–25
, Skinning	24–25
Stock	25
Flaky Pastry	86–87
Flans	96–97
Flemish Stew	38
Fluffy Chocolate Semolina	75
Freezing Fruit and Vegetables	124–125
French Beans Vinaigrette	53

Beef Stew	38
Omelette	15
Salad Dressing	53
Fresh Lemonade	117
Fried Eggs	14
Fish	28
Frikadeller	43
Fritters	17
Fruit	82–83
and Vegetables, Bottling	122–123
and Vegetables, Freezing	124–125
Batter Pudding	17
Biscuits	111
Cakes	104–105
Crumble	80–81
Flans	96
Fool	83
Ice Cream	72
Puddings, Baked	80–81
Salad, Golden	83
Sauce, Thick	65
Scones	99
, Stewed	83
Suet Pudding	77
Tea Bread and Buns	114–115
Fruity Apple Dumplings	85
Frying and Grilling Meat and Poultry	36–37

G

Gaspacho	13
Gelatine, Cold Desserts with	70
Ginger Beer	117
Nuts	111
Gingerbread	103
Glacé Icing	108
Glühwein	117
Golden Fruit Salad	83
Syrup Buns	103
Grilled Cheesy Cod Cutlets	29
Fish	28
Grilling, Frying and, Meat and Poultry	36–37
Green Tomato Chutney	120

H

Hawaiian Pineapple Pie	97
Heavenly Cheesecake	69
Herbed Marinade	47
Rice	56
Herbs and Spices	8–9
Herring Roes on Toast	25
Herrings, Soused	31
Hollandaise Sauce	60–61
Honeycombe Mould	71
Honey Ball Flan	73
Walnut Scones	99
Horseradish Sauce	62
Hot Cheese Soufflé	21
Puddings	74–81
Puddings, Freezer tip	79
Soufflés	21
Water Crust Pastry	90–91

I

Ice Cream	72–73
Icings and Fillings, Cakes	108–109
Irish Stew	39

J

Jam Pancakes	17
Suet Pudding	77
Jams and Marmalades	118–119
Jelly, Orange Egg	70

K

Kedgeree	31
Kidneys, Devilled	44

L

Lamb and Vegetable Pie	95
, Buying	33
, Casseroled	38
, Curried	38
, Frying and Grilling	36

, Irish Stew 39
, Roast 34
Lardy Cake 115
Lasagne 55
Lemonade, Fresh 117
Lemon Delicious Pudding 79
Honey Tea Cake 102
Mousse or Soufflé 66
Pancakes 17
Sauce 64
Liver and Bacon Casserole 44
Pâté 44
Lobster 26

M

Macaroni Cheese 55
Marinades, Stuffings and 46–47
Marmalade, Jams and 118–119
Suet Pudding 77
Mayonnaise 61
Meat 32–47
, Boiling 40–41
, Buying 32–33
, Freezer Note 41
, Frying and Grilling 36–37
, Minced 42, 43
, Offal 44–45
, Roast 34–35
, Stews and Casseroles 38–39
Meaty Pancakes 17
Meringue Nests or Baskets 20
Topping 21
Meringues 20–21
Milk Shake, Strawberry 117
Milky Puddings, Hot 74–75
Minced Meat 42–43
Mint Sauce 62
Mixed Grill 37
Mornay Sauce 59
Mousses and Cold Soufflés 66–67
Mushrooms, Chicken with 39
Salad 53
Mussels 27

O

Offal Dishes 44–45
Omelettes 14–15
Onion Rice 56
Onions, Pickled 121
Orange Egg Jelly 70
Flummery, Apricot 71
Sauce 64
Water Ice 73
Oysters 26

P

Pancakes 17
, Scotch 99
Paprika Pork 39
Parsley and Thyme Stuffing 46
Sauce 59
Pasta and Rice 54–57
, Freezer Note 57
Pastry 84–97
, Choux 92–93
, Flaky 86–87
, Freezer Note 89
, Hot water crust 90–91
, Rough Puff 87
, Shortcrust 84–85
, Suet Crust 88–89
Pâté, Liver 44
Peppers, Stuffed 49
Pickles, Chutneys and 120–121
Pickled Onions 121
Pies, Raised 90–91
Sweet and Savoury 94–95
Pineapple Lemon Upside Down Pudding 79
Pie, Hawaiian 97
Plain Fruit Cake 104
Plum Jam 119
Poached Eggs 14
Fish 28

Pork, Buying 33
, Casseroled 39
, Chinese 39
, Frying and Grilling 36
, Paprika 39
, Roast 35
, Spiced Pressed 41
Potato Salad 53
Soup 11
Potatoes, Baked in their Jackets 51
, Casseroled 51
, Duchesse 51
Poultry, Buying 33
, Frying and Grilling 37
, Roast 38
Prawns 26
Preserving 118–125
Puddings, Baked Fruit 80–81
, Hot 74–81
, Sponge 78
, Steamed Suet 76

Q

Quick and Easy Ice Cream 72
Mix Sponge Sandwich 101

R

Raspberry Jam 119
Mousse or Soufflé 67
Ratatouille 49
Rhubarb Charlotte 81
Rice 56–57
, Pudding, Baked 74–75
Rich Fruit Cake 105
Risotto 57
Roast Meat and Poultry 34
Rock Cakes 103
Roes on Toast, Herring 25
Root Vegetables 50–51
Rough Puff Pastry 87
Royal Icing 109
Rubbed-in and Gingerbread cake mixtures 102–103

S

Sage and Onion Stuffing 46
Salad Dressing, French 53
Vegetables 52–53
Salad Niçoise 53
Sauce, Bolognese 55
, Egg Custard 18
Sauces 58–65
for Main Dishes 62–63
, Savoury Egg Based 60–61
, Sweet 64
Thickened with Flour, Savoury 58–59
Sausage Rolls, Bacon 87
Savoury Egg Based Sauces 60–61
Scallops 26
Scones 98–99
Scotch Pancakes 99
Scrambled Eggs 14
Seafood Cocktail Sauce 61
Semolina, Fluffy Chocolate 75
Seville Orange Marmalade 119
Shellfish 26–27
Shepherds Pie 42
Shortcrust Pastry 84–85
Short-time White Bread 112
Shrimps 26
Soufflé Omelette 15
Soufflés, Cold 66–67
, Hot 21
Soups 10–13
, Freezing 13
Soused Herring 31
Spanish Chicken 39
Flan 97
Omelette 15
Speedy Wheatmeal Bread 113
Spiced Pressed Pork 41
Vinegar 120
Spices, Herbs and 8–9

Spicy Scones 99
Sponge Puddings 78
Steak, Kidney and Mushroom Pudding 88
Steamed Suet Puddings 76
Stewed Fruit 83
Stews and Casseroles 38–39
Stock, Meat and Poultry 11
, Fish 25
Strawberry Jam 118
Layer Cake 107
Milk Shake 117
Syllabub 69
Stuffed Peppers 49
Stuffings and Marinades 46–47
Suet Crust Pastry 88–89
Pudding, Steamed 76
Summer Pudding 83
Sweet and Savoury Pies 94–95
Sauces 64–65
White Sauce 64
Swiss Roll 106–107
Syllabub, Strawberry 69
Syrup Pudding, Coconut 78
Roly Poly 89

T

Tartare Sauce 61
Tea Scones 99
Thick Fruit Sauce 65
Three Fruit Marmalade 119
Toad in the Hole 17
Tomato Chutney, Green 120
Sauce 63
Soup 12
Vinaigrette 53
Treacle Scone 99
Trifle, Family Apricot 68

U

Upside Down Pudding, Pineapple Lemon 79

V

Veal, Buying 33
Ham and Egg Pie 90–91
, Roast 34
Vegetables, Bottling Fruit and 122–123
, Buying and Cooking Fresh 48–53
, Freezer Note 53
, Freezing Fruit and 124–125
, Root 50–51
, Salad 52–53
Victoria Sandwich 101
Vinegar, Spiced 120

W

Whelks 27
Whisked Cakes 106–107
White Coating Sauce 58
Wholewheat Scones 99
Winkles 27

Y

Yeast, Cooking with 112–115
Yoghourt 68–69
Marinade 47

127

Acknowledgements

The author would like to thank the following for the colour pictures in this book and also for allowing their material to be used for artwork references.

Cover picture, Spanish Chicken, by courtesy of **Olives from Spain**

Model, Carolyn Bedford/Sackett Publishing Services Ltd.

Cover picture and pictures on page 19, 55, 68, 70, 74, 104, 112, 116 by **Robert Glover Studio**

Bejam News

Making Celery Soup	12
Making a Cheese Slice	23
Making Fish Nicoise	29
Barbecue Marinade	47
Making Stuffed Peppers	48–49
Making Chicken and Rice Salad Ring	57
Making Espagnole Sauce	59
Making Apricot Pie	94–95
Preparing apples for freezing	124

British Egg Information Service

Souffle Omelette	15
Making Pancakes	17

British Meat Service

Carcases and cuts of meat	32–33
Roast Lamb	34
Mixed Grill	37
Spiced Pressed Pork	41
Liver and Bacon Casserole	45
Steak, Kidney and Mushroom Pudding	88

Cadbury Typhoo Ltd

Chocolate Sauce on Pears and Ice Cream	65
Chocolate Orange Mousse	67
Cream Buns	93

Colmans Mustard

Cheese Straws	84
Dried Apricot Chutney	120

The Danish Food Centre

Danish Blue Cauliflower Cheese	23

Dutch Dairy Bureau

Cheese Omelette	15
Kedgeree	31

Gales Honey

Meringue-topped pudding	20
Honey Ball Flan	73
Honey Walnut Scones	98
Honied Butter Icing	108

Herring Industry Board

Soused Herrings	31

Kraft Foods Ltd

Making Scrambled Eggs	15
Making Baked Egg Custard	18–19
Preparing Fish	25
Dressing a crab	27
Making Mayonnaise	61
Making a Sweet White Sauce	64
Making a Cold Soufflé	66
Making Shortcrust Pastry	85
Making Flaky Pastry	87
Lining a pudding basin with pastry	89
Making Gingerbread	103
Making a Swiss Roll	107

Olives from Spain

Gaspacho	13
Spanish Chicken	39
Salade Niçoise	52
Spanish Flan	97

Potato Marketing Board

Shepherds Pie	42
Baked Potatoes in their Jackets	51

Tate and Lyle Ltd

Cheese Soufflé	21
Butterscotch Sundae	73
Coconut Syrup Pudding	78
Baked Apples	80
Golden Fruit Salad	82
Gingerbread	102
Biscuits	110

Tower Housewares Ltd

Potato Soup	11
Making a Cheese Soufflé	21
Preparing and Roasting a Turkey	35
Making Pâté	44
Ratatouille	49
Hollandaise Sauce	60
Making a Veal, Ham and Egg Pie	90–91
Making Choux Pastry	92–93
Making a flan case	96
Making a Victoria Sandwich	100–101
Breads and Buns	114

The Tupperware Company

Preparing strawberries and French beans for freezing	125

The White Fish Kitchen

Fish Cakes	30

Tableware and accessories for the pictures on pages 19, 55, 68, 74, 104, 112, 116 by Midas Ltd, Westerham, Kent